Managing
Your Career

HBR WORKING PARENTS SERIES

Tips, stories, and strategies for the job that never ends.

The **HBR Working Parents Series** supports readers as they anticipate challenges, learn how to advocate for themselves more effectively, juggle their impossible schedules, and find fulfillment at home and at work.

From classic issues such as work-life balance and making time for yourself to thorny challenges such as managing an urgent family crisis and the impact of parenting on your career, this series features the practical tips, strategies, and research you need to be—and feel—more effective at home and at work. Whether you're up with a newborn or touring universities with your teen, we've got what you need to make working parenthood work for you.

Books in the series include:

Advice for Working Dads

Advice for Working Moms

Communicate Better with Everyone

Getting It All Done

Managing Your Career

Taking Care of Yourself

WORKING PARENTS

*Tips, stories, and
strategies for the job
that never ends.*

Managing
Your Career

Harvard Business
Review Press
Boston, Massachusetts

Copyright 2021 Harvard Business School Publishing Corporation
All rights reserved
Printed in the United States of America

10 9 8 7 6 5 4 3 2 1

The web addresses referenced in this book were live and correct at the time of the book's publication but may be subject to change.

Cataloging-in-Publication data is forthcoming.

ISBN: 978-1-63369-972-4
eISBN: 978-1-63369-973-1

The paper used in this publication meets the requirements of the American National Standard for Permanence of Paper for Publications and Documents in Libraries and Archives Z39.48-1992.

CONTENTS

Contents

Section 4

Without GPS

Navigate on and off the Career Ramp

Section 6

Don't Go It Alone

Get Support

Contents

Epilogue

To Infinity, and Beyond!

It happens just as fast as people say.

by Avivah Wittenberg-Cox

INTRODUCTION

The Same, but Completely Different

by Daisy Dowling

I had just been offered a dream job: the chance to kick-start a career-development and coaching service inside a big, growing, financially healthy organization, working with people I liked. The gig would come with a higher salary, a ton of senior exposure, and a swank midtown office. It was just the kind of juicy, good-from-every-angle career opportunity I'd been hoping for.

But was I *really* ready to leave a comfortable job at a great company to leap into the unknown when, as a parent of a young child, I had crazy-big responsibilities at home? (You know the ones I'm talking about.) Even if I were poised to take that risk, I didn't have any sponsors or supporters at Dream Co., and I'd have to work much longer hours to prove myself, which meant more time away from my family. This kind of job didn't come along often, and these days I wasn't networking or getting out on the job market very much. And as my daughter grew, I wanted to spend even more time with her, so *that* wasn't going to change anytime soon.

I was spinning: mentally careening between home and work, work and home, with what felt like hundreds of hopes and pressures and intentions attached to each. Despite earning my living as a career and leadership expert, I didn't know how to fulfill my own professional interests and ambitions while being the loving, present parent I wanted to be. I felt confused and alone.

Of course, I wasn't. Every working parent faces this daunting, unexplained, and complex phase of professional life when we're not just building our careers—but *building our careers as working parents*. Maybe you've just welcomed your first child and are trying to figure out a workable schedule. Or you've got older kids and want to pedal-to-the-metal it—or take a break or make a change—in your professional life but aren't sure how. Maybe you don't have a lot of working-parent role models in your field or organization. Maybe the flextime or sponsorship that a new mom might ask for doesn't feel accessible for you as a dad, a parent of an older kid, a member of an LGBTQ+ family, or a foster parent. Or perhaps all the standard practices you've used to push yourself forward professionally don't seem to be working so well now.

Whatever the specifics, I can assure you you're not alone—I see evidence of that every day in my role as career coach to working parents. I've yet to meet one who has an innate, clear view of how to fit career and family together. The kid-plus-career challenge is so complex, individual, and dynamic that there are no silver bullets; it can't be solved through intuition or with any single approach or system. So, don't beat yourself up. You're not the problem—the problem is the problem. We're *all* grappling with this.

Here's my favorite big-picture way to make that grappling seem a little easier. Try thinking about general career management just as you would good nutrition. It's essential to your professional health, at every phase. Kids or no kids, you can't build a great career without self-advocacy, networking, good communication, sufficient risk taking, soliciting feedback, and so on. But when you become a parent, you need to change your diet, just a little: You'll want to start seasoning your food more to taste, so that it suits *you*. Parental leaves, flex work, time-management hacks, new forms of communication, boundary setting—to name just a few of the tricks and tools of working parenthood—help you do so. Pair career-management basics with the right combination of those extras and blend and adjust as needed to create a satisfying working-parent-career dish. "Working parent career management" isn't an either/or—it's about bringing new elements into the mix.

This book is your tool for finding that successful, satisfying combination both today and over the long term. Full disclosure: If you want a comprehensive career how-to, look elsewhere, and if a manifesto on the rights of working parents is what you're after, this isn't it. But if you want to understand the essential ingredients of a successful working-parent career, then keep right on reading—and come back to these pages often. If you realize that you've fallen into the common trap of working too much and not being adequately visible career-wise, David Burkus's "Making Time for Networking as a Working Parent" will give you a gentle nudge and some practical ways to build on the contacts you already have. When all that good networking leads to a terrific job offer, Amy Gallo's "Winning Support for Flexible Work" or Jennifer Petriglieri's "How Dual-Career Couples Make It Work" can help you take that next step in a way that works for your unique family situation. Walled off the two spheres of your life? Try the "crossover" strategy advised in Scott Edinger's "The Family 360 Review."

Whatever the specifics of your home life or career, this book will help you develop greater confidence and more of a plan, and it will point you toward great ideas for new paths to take and new approaches to try. And that's precisely what you, and I, and *every* busy professional mom and dad needs.

Section 1

Oh, the Places You'll Go!

Take Stock and Set Your Vision

How to Build a Meaningful Career

by Amy Gallo

Quick Takes

- Set your own definition of *meaningful*
- Identify things you're good at and enjoy doing
- Consider your ideal salary, benefits, and schedule
- Imagine possible roles and create experiments to test them
- Think about where you want to be in 5, 10, 20 years
- Make a budget to give yourself a financial buffer

veryone aspires to have purpose or meaning in their career, but it isn't always easy to find, especially when you have obligations to consider. Building a career that helps you meet your family responsibilities *and* feeds your soul is challenging but not impossible. What practical steps can you take to make sure you're not just toiling away for a paycheck but doing something you genuinely care about?

What the Experts Say

Unfortunately, most of us don't know how to make the job decisions that lead to satisfaction, regardless of our family situation. Nathaniel Koloc, the CEO of ReWork, which provides recruiting services to companies that offer purposeful work, says that's because no one really ever teaches us how: "Very few parents, teachers, and mentors urge us to think about this or give us mental models to use," he says. As a result, we often pick jobs for the wrong reasons, says Karen Dillon, coauthor of *How Will You Measure Your Life?* "We look for things that we're proud to talk about at a cocktail party or look good on a résumé." But rarely are those the things that translate to satisfaction. Here are principles you can follow to find a career—and a specific job—you love that's not good just for you, but for your family, too.

Know what "meaningful" means to you

Am I respected by my colleagues? Am I being challenged? Am I growing? Do I believe in the mission? Am I proud of the work I do? "These are the things that are going to make the difference between being OK with your job and being truly happy," says Dillon. But "meaningful" means something different for each of us. "Don't just look to obvious things, like salary, title, or prestige of the company," says Dillon. Koloc identifies four categories to consider.

Legacy. This is about the concrete outcomes of your work. What do you want to achieve? Sure, you may spend a lot of your day responding to emails or attending meetings, but what evidence do you want of your work? What do you want to look back on and know you accomplished? What do you want your children to remember about the work you did? You might find it rewarding to advance the math skills of 80 students in one year or build six desalination plants over the course of your career. This is often a question of how close to the front lines you want to be. Some people want to help sick people directly, while others aspire to help pass policies that will give more people access to health care.

Mastery. These are the strengths that you want to improve. For example, if you enjoy connecting with people, you could use that skill to be a psychologist or a marketer. If you're a strong writer, you could use that skill to write fiction or ad copy. The key is that you're using your strengths in a way that you find rewarding. "Being good at something you don't enjoy doesn't count," says Koloc. "It has to be something you love to do."

Freedom. This is about the salary, benefits, and flexibility you need to live the life you want. For some people, this may mean a big paycheck that allows you to take your family on exotic vacations or to afford music lessons for your children. For others, it could be the freedom to work when and where you choose. Many working parents want the ability to work from home when a child or partner is sick, or the flexibility to take an hour or two during the workday to attend a school event. Others want to know they can be home for dinner with their family or accompany an aging parent on a doctor's visit, when necessary. Consider the lifestyle you want and ask whether your job is helping you fulfill that.

Alignment. This last category covers the culture and values of the place where you work. This is not the same as mission, warns Koloc, but is about whether you feel as if you belong. What are the beliefs and priorities of the company and the people you work with? How do people treat one another? Are there other working parents there whom you can turn to for support? Does the organization offer community service days? Do colleagues eat lunch together? "It's important to enjoy spending time with your colleagues and your manager," says Dillon. The content of these categories will vary by person. Dillon suggests making a list of all the things you value and then prioritizing them. This list will help guide your decisions and can be used to evaluate specific opportunities like a new assignment in your current role, a job at a different company, or a new career path.

Form hypotheses

If you're unsure what matters most to you, think through a given day or week at work. Ask yourself: What made me most happy on the job? What did I find most frustrating? Then, Koloc suggests, come up with a few hypotheses about what is most meaningful to you. *I want a job where I create something that people can use every day. I want a job that allows me enough flexibility to pick up my kids from school three days a week. I want a job where I'm directly interacting with people in need.* "Be careful not to overcorrect for a particularly bad job experience," says Dillon. "When you have a micromanaging boss, for example, it's easy to think that your biggest priority is to work for a manager who doesn't smother you, but if you seek out that one thing, you may end up being unhappy for slightly different reasons."

Run experiments

Once you've nailed down your hypotheses, it's time to test them. There are a variety of ways to do this. First, you can try things out within an existing job. "You might convince your manager to let you work remotely for a month," he says. Take on a new assignment that allows you to build new skills. "Look for opportunities to enhance your job. Sign up for a new cross-company initiative or propose taking something off your boss's plate," suggests Dillon. If you can't run experiments within the constraints of your job, look outside the company. "Join industry groups, go to conferences, volunteer for a nonprofit," advises Dillon. The third way to test your hypotheses is to have conversations. Find people who are doing what you think you want to do and ask them lots of questions. Ideally these will be folks whose involvement with their family and community is similar to yours, so they can reflect on how possible it is to do the job you aspire to and meet your family commitments. Listen carefully and critically, so that you don't just hear what you want to hear.

Form a personal "board of directors"

Don't go it alone. Work with others to kick the tires on your hypotheses and share the results of your experiments. Invite four or five people to serve as your informal board of directors, making sure to include a few fellow working parents who understand the realities of your life (see chapter 17). You might tell them, "I'm doing some exploring about what I want from work and I'd love to talk with you on occasion to get your feedback on my direction." Include any mentors and trusted professional peers. And if your manager is receptive, include her as well. "Not all bosses may be supportive," says Dillon, "but if you have a manager whom you can bounce career ideas off of, take advantage of that."

There are a few people you shouldn't include, says Koloc. "Family members can be tough," says Koloc. "Spouses, for example, need to know what you're doing, but they may not be best positioned to help you figure it out."

Think long term

This work shouldn't just be in service of getting your next job. "Career design is different than a job-search strategy," says Koloc, and the question you should be asking yourself, he advises, is not "What job do I want?" but "What life do I want?" Think about where you want to be in 5, 10,

20 years. Consider what type of relationship you'd like to have with your family as your children grow up. Talk to colleagues and friends who have children who are older than yours to help you anticipate what types of challenges you may face as a parent later on in your career. Of course, you have to answer more-immediate questions about what you want in your current job or your next, but do so only in the context of your longer, larger career goals.

When you're already deep into a career

Midcareer professionals can and do make big changes—even those with rent and college tuition to pay. "Your ability to turn the ship is no different, but the speed at which you turn it is going to be slower," says Koloc. "If you're 35 and have two kids, it's going to take longer to explore." There's good news though, he says: "You have more clues as to what you want and enjoy." The important thing is to not feel stuck. "You may feel locked into a job, a higher salary, a higher title because you have more responsibilities, like a mortgage and kids, and sure, you may need to take fewer risks, but you don't want to settle for a job or career you're not happy with," says Dillon.

Buckle down on your finances

One of the main reasons people give for staying in a job or career they don't love is money. "Take steps to give yourself a financial cushion and a little psychological freedom," says Dillon. Make a budget if you don't have one. Look for ways to lower the amount of money you need each month: Downsize your house, move to one car, and be more disciplined about saving. Involve your family in this effort, making sure everyone in your household is on the same page about reducing spending and the reason behind it. Having a financial buffer will make it more likely that when you find something meaningful, you'll be able to act on it.

Make the time

"I have yet to meet anybody who wouldn't benefit from setting aside dedicated time to sit down and think about what they want from work," says Koloc. Schedule a time in your calendar to reflect on your career. While it can be difficult to find room in an already full schedule, even if it's just an hour every other week, you're going to make some progress. If you have older kids, you might even involve them in the process, asking them to also reflect on what a meaningful career will look like for them in the future. "Sometimes just thinking about it will get the ball rolling, and then, often, the change becomes inevitable," says Koloc.

Case Study: Get Your Finances in Order

Tim Groves liked his job at a civil litigation law firm. But he didn't love it. "I didn't get up in the morning excited to go to work," he says. "And I knew if I continued on that career path, it wasn't going to get better either." Making a career change wasn't straightforward, given that he didn't want to do anything to jeopardize his current job or his ability to provide for his family while searching for another role. He was interested in mission-driven work, so he started by talking to people in the nonprofit world and signed up for automated job listings. "I volunteered and served on boards, and I had friends and relatives who worked in nonprofits, so I had an inkling of what I could do with a law degree in a nonprofit setting," he says.

He also did a few informational interviews with people he respected who had made similar transitions. He was careful in how he set up these conversations. "I told people that I wasn't miserable at my current job, but that I was looking around and would love their perspective," he explains. "I also mentioned that I had a mortgage and a family, so I didn't want to broadcast this."

To broaden his network, he became more active in his volunteer and board work and upped the pro bono law work he was doing. "I put myself in contact with people who could connect me to an opportunity or who could vouch for me when an opportunity came up."

Tim and his wife had supported each other through several career transitions, but this time, as he says, "the stakes were higher because we had kids, school tuitions, and college looming on the horizon." Given that Tim was going to almost certainly take a pay cut, he and his wife came up with a budget and the lowest salary figure he could take. To give themselves more financial flexibility, they downsized and moved from a one-family to a two-family house where rent from tenants could help pay the mortgage.

About a year and a half after starting the process, Tim took a job as a development officer at the Rhode Island Foundation. "The process wasn't always easy, but I feel good about where I ended up," he says.

Adapted from content posted on hbr.org, February 4, 2015 (product #H01V4K).

Work + Home + Community + Self

by Stewart D. Friedman

Quick Takes

- Don't balance; integrate the main aspects of your life

- Know what matters most to you

- Consider how you can use your skills in different roles

- Small shifts can give you big energy boosts

- Tap your most creative friends

O vercommitted. Distracted. Stressed out. Stretched too thin. This is how many of us describe ourselves today. I hear it from men and women; from the young and the old; from executives, MBA students, doctors, retailers, artisans, research scientists, soldiers, stay-at-home parents, teachers, and engineers around the world. In an age of constant communication and economic pressure, everyone is struggling to have meaningful work, domestic bliss, community engagement, and a satisfying inner life. Some have already given up on the idea of having it all: As I discovered in 2013 in a study comparing undergraduates from the classes of 1992 and 2012 at the University of Pennsylvania's Wharton School, a significant number of Millennials (the generation born from 1980 to 2000) are deciding not to become parents, because they don't see how they can fit children into their busy lives.

A commitment to better work-life balance isn't the solution. As I've argued for a long time—and as many more people are now asserting—balance is bunk. It's a misguided metaphor because it assumes we must always make trade-offs among the four main aspects of our lives: work or school, home or family (however you define that), community (friends, neighbors, religious or social groups), and self (mind, body, spirit). A more realistic and more gratifying goal is better *integration* between work and the rest of life through the pursuit of *four-way wins*, which improve performance in all four dimensions.

Such integration starts with embracing three key principles—be real, be whole, and be innovative—that I described in a 2008 HBR article, "Be a Better Leader, Have a Richer Life." It takes certain skills to bring those principles to life. In my 30 years as a professor, researcher, consultant, and executive, as I've studied and served thousands of people, I've found 18 specific skills that foster greater alignment and harmony among the four life domains. In this article I describe those skills and offer exercises—drawn from the latest findings in organizational psychology and related fields—to help you hone a few of the skills that business professionals often find most difficult to master. While there's more you can do to instill the three principles (you'll find a wider range of exercises in my book, *Leading the Life You Want: Skills for Integrating Work and Life*), the advice offered here will help you move down the right path.

Skills for Being Real

For well over a decade I've run a program called Total Leadership that teaches the three principles to executives,

MBA candidates, and many others. It starts with a focus on being real—how to act with authenticity by clarifying what's important, wherever you are, whatever you're doing. That requires you to:

- Know what matters

- Embody values consistently

- Align actions with values

- Convey values with stories

- Envision your legacy

- Hold yourself accountable

The ability to do the first two things is especially crucial. Let's begin with how to know what matters. One exercise that enhances this skill, called *four circles*, has you examine the importance and congruence of your various roles and responsibilities in life. (You can do it online at this free site: www.myfourcircles.com.) You start by drawing circles representing the four domains—work, home, community, and self—varying the sizes to reflect how much you value each. Next you move the circles to show whether and to what degree they overlap. At this point you think about the values, goals, interests, actions, and results you pursue in each domain. Are they compatible or in opposition? Imagine what your life would be like if your aspirations in all four circles, and the means by which you achieved them, lined up perfectly, like the concentric rings of a tree trunk. For most of us that's an unattainable ideal, but what actions could you realistically take to move toward that kind of overlap? Could you change how you work, or even how you think about the purpose of your work, without diminishing the personal value you derive from it? Could you help your family to better see how your business life benefits them so that they would be more supportive of it?

A complementary exercise, called *conversation starter*, encourages people to embody values consistently. This involves bringing an object from your nonwork life (such as a family photograph, a travel memento, or a trophy) into the office. If a colleague mentions it, you explain what this part of your life means to you *and* how it helps you at work. Then you consider asking that person to bring their own conversation starter. You might also take something from your work to your home and talk to your roommates, spouse, kids, or dinner guests about it. Tell them about what you do and who you are in your role at work, focusing especially on what this might mean for them.

When Victoria, the head of marketing for a pharmaceutical company division, drew her four circles, she initially placed the biggest one, representing work, apart from all the rest. She didn't see any real connection between her professional identity and her home, community, and inner lives. But when she began to talk about the separation with a few colleagues, friends, and family members, she came to realize that one major aspect of her mission as an executive—promoting greater health—was a lot more compatible with her other circles than she had thought.

She could also see how just a few small changes in approach might create much more overlap. For example, at home she started to talk more with her two daughters about the social impact of her business, sharing stories about all the ways in which her company's medicines were saving lives. The girls responded with greater pride in, and understanding of, their mom's commitment to work. As a team leader, Victoria began to reframe core drug-marketing tasks in terms of the products' benefits to end users—who were all the children, spouses, parents, siblings, friends, or neighbors of someone—just like the families and communities she and her employees had. As a result, her group became more impassioned and hardworking, which ultimately eased her load and gave her more time for other pursuits. Perhaps most important, Victoria felt less guilt about the way she was spending her time and energy, and newly secure in her mission at the office as well as in her family's support.

Skills for Being Whole

The second principle that Total Leadership addresses is being whole—or acting with integrity. What I mean by that is respecting the fact that all the roles you play make up one whole person and encouraging others to view you the same way. To do that you must be able to:

- Clarify expectations

- Help others

- Build supportive networks

- Apply all your resources

- Manage boundaries intelligently

- Weave disparate strands

One of the most important skills here is knowing how to apply all your resources (such as your knowledge, skills, and contacts) in the various domains of your life to benefit the other domains. An exercise that helps you do that is called *talent transfer*. It involves writing a résumé listing all the skills you've developed—from mentoring colleagues, organizing family activities, or running a church bake sale—and thinking of how each might be used to achieve different ends. Organizational psychologists call this a strength-development approach: You identify your talents and then apply them in new areas, enhancing them further. Another way to do this is to reflect on something that makes you feel good—a work accomplishment, a fruitful friendship, your commitment to salsa dancing—and then consider an area of your life you'd like to improve. How might the skills you used to achieve the former help you in the latter?

To manage boundaries intelligently is another key challenge. I advise people to practice something I call *segment and merge,* and then decide which strategy works best when. First, think about ways to create separation (in time and space) between your different roles. You might try setting limits on yourself. For example, if there's an ambitious work project that you've been putting off, try dedicating the first two hours of each Saturday morning for the next month to tackling it, and then give yourself the rest of the day off. Or, if your job keeps monopolizing your evenings, you might experiment with a "no smartphones at the dinner table" policy. Now do the opposite: Think about opportunities to bring together two or more parts of your life. You might take a child to a company-sponsored charity run or bring a coworker to a block party in your neighborhood. After you've tried a new way of segmenting and a new way of merging, jot down your insights about what worked and what didn't, for both you and the people around you. Were you more or less productive? Did you find yourself more or less distracted? How did others react? Were they put off, or did they seem to feel closer to and more trusting of you?

An example of the segmenting concept in action comes from Brian, a manager in an accounting firm. In a monthlong experiment, he set aside his 40-minute train rides to and from work solely for "downtime." He caught up on emails to family and friends and invested in his own development through reading and reflection—for example, by diagramming the factors affecting his sense of stability, including his stress and energy levels and his feelings about himself, his relationships, and his future. Sometimes, as an alternative to that inward focus, he had conversations with the neighbors, colleagues, and acquaintances he sat next to on the train, exchanging advice about everything from childcare to real estate. This simple reallocation of commuting time—from doing work to other things—resulted, perhaps paradoxically, in Brian's being better prepared for work and more proactive about his career progression. He also felt closer to his extended family and the old friends with whom he'd reconnected and to the people in his local community, because he was engaging with more of them on his way to the office and back. Having an after-work buffer period allowed him to reenter his home with less stress and more openness and to develop new insights about how he could be a better father and husband. Personally, he also felt "more grounded and less crazed." He came to see more clearly the positive impact of rest and recovery on his performance, which led him to experiment with increasing his sleep time by about an hour a day. Again, the small shift in boundaries significantly boosted his productivity, well-being, and relationships. Everyone with whom he interacted daily noticed that he was less cranky and more energetic.

Skills for Being Innovative

The third Total Leadership principle is to be innovative—to act with creativity in identifying and pursuing more four-way wins. To do so, you need to:

- Focus on results

- Resolve conflicts among domains

- Challenge the status quo

- See new ways of doing things

- Embrace change courageously

- Create cultures of innovation around you

Scenario exercises are one of several effective methods of increasing your capacity to focus on results, especially on the quality of your contributions rather than the amount of time or energy you spend on them. Scenarios involve identifying a specific goal you want to achieve and then listing three alternative ways to get there, including the resources you'll need and the challenges you'll face. This sort of brainstorming encourages you to keep your eyes on the prize. Another method is experimenting with new patterns of behavior, trying activities at new times or in different places. It could be something as simple as shaving at the gym instead of at home, or practicing your trumpet at the office after hours rather than disturbing your neighbors at home. What were the pros and cons of switching up your routine? How did it affect your results?

Crowdsourcing is an exercise that helps you practice how to see new ways of doing things. To try this, gather a group of your most creative friends and describe a problem you're facing. Then ask for ideas about potential solutions and record what you hear. Select the one you think wisest, draft a plan, and try to make it happen. Stay in touch with your advisers, at least weekly, and after a month or so review your results with them. If the approach you tried didn't work, or if you need more time to solve the problem, tweak your behavior or try another idea altogether, drawing on what you learned from the first experiment.

Former Bain & Company CEO Tom Tierney took not months but years to think about and solicit advice on what would eventually become the Bridgespan Group—an independent nonprofit that was incubated in and then spun out of Bain—which provides strategic consulting and leadership development to philanthropists, foundations, and other nonprofit organizations. In the 1980s he began to think, write, and talk about his idea for what he then generically called "Make a Difference Company," picking the brains of colleagues and friends, including the likes of the presidential adviser and founder of Common Cause, John Gardner. Emboldened by those conversations, Tierney at first took small steps to move closer to his vision by, for example, volunteering for the United Way of the Bay Area while he was running Bain's San Francisco office and eventually joining the nonprofit's board. This was the first of many on which he would serve. In 1999, Tierney folded all that experience, knowledge, and crowdsourced wisdom into Bridgespan, and a year later he stepped down as chief executive of Bain to focus on the new organization. Leading the life you want is a craft. As with music, writing, dance, or any athletic endeavor, you can always get better at it by practicing. That's why I developed these exercises and many others. Start with these three big ideas: Be real, be whole, and be innovative. Understand the skills you need to accomplish each. And then commit to doing the fun and fruitful work of making them part of your leadership repertoire.

Reprinted from Harvard Business Review, *September 2014 (product #R1409K).*

Section 2

Be All Ears

Get Feedback

Get the Feedback You Need

by Carolyn O'Hara

Quick Takes

- Understand your strengths
- Focus your limited time for professional development
- Check in on how you did in the moment
- Ask, "What's one thing I could improve?"
- Probe for specifics

You need feedback to learn and grow, and if you're waiting for your annual review to find out how you're performing, you're not getting enough of it. But how do you get the focused input you need? And if your boss is stingy with pointers and advice, how do you encourage them to give you more? Who else should you be asking to help you improve?

What the Experts Say

Receiving feedback can be "a stressful experience," says Ed Batista, an executive coach and an instructor at the Stanford Graduate School of Business. That's why many people hesitate to ask for it. But the more often you do, the less stressful it becomes to initiate the conversation and to hear the comments. "If you're having a feedback conversation every week, there's less to be surprised by and more opportunity to modify your behavior," Batista explains. The process will also make you happier and more productive at work, adds Sheila Heen, author of *Thanks for the Feedback: The Science and Art of Receiving Feedback Well.* "People who go out and solicit negative feedback—meaning they aren't just fishing for compliments—report higher satisfaction," she says. "They adapt more quickly to new roles, get higher performance reviews, and show others they are committed to doing their jobs." Here's how to ask for feedback that helps you get ahead.

Understand what you're looking for

Think about the kind of feedback you crave. Do you want more appreciation or acknowledgment? Evaluation of your performance on a particular project or task? Or general coaching about how you can improve and learn? Knowing this will help you craft your approach, says Heen. "You can go to your boss and say, 'I feel like I get a ton of appreciation around here. I know I'm valued. What I don't have a sense of is what I need to work on.'" And while advice on areas in which you can develop is often the most useful, "there is value in asking for positive feedback as well," says Batista. Don't hesitate to ask your boss to review your performance on an obviously successful project. "It can be an opportunity to build a stronger relationship," he says.

Ask for feedback in real time

If you want some insight into how you did on a particular task or how you might improve on the next project, don't dawdle. It's best to ask sooner rather than later. Batista advises that you not try to do it all in one conversation. "Chop it up into manageable chunks and space out the interactions," he says. You also don't have to schedule time in advance or make a formal approach. "Don't think of it as sitting down to have an official conversation," says Heen. "Just reach out to your boss, colleagues, or clients and have a very quick and informal coaching exchange." You might pull your boss aside after a meeting or close a conversation with a client with a parting request for their reaction to your role on a recent project.

Pose specific questions

Whatever you do, don't start off by asking, "Do you have any feedback for me?" "That's a terrible question," says Heen. "The answer is almost always no and you learn nothing." She recommends instead asking, "What's one thing I could improve?" so it's clear that you're asking for coaching and it's clear that you assume there's at least one thing you can work on. You can also tailor the question to the specific situation: "What's one thing I could have done better in that meeting or presentation?" You should also avoid asking questions that are likely to result in yes- or no- answers. "Asking questions that begin with 'how' or 'what' will elicit fuller responses," Batista says. He suggests questions like, "How did that go from your perspective?" or "What do you think I might have done differently?"

Press for examples

To get the most out of the feedback you receive, you may have to ask for specifics. "Sometimes, the person will say, 'I just think you need to be more assertive or more proactive or more of a team player,'" says Heen. "That's vague and what we call a label. It's not very helpful. You have to unpack the label." To do that, ask probing questions like, "Can you explain what you mean?" "How could I have been more assertive just now?" and "What kinds of things should I do to be more assertive going forward?"

Turn to colleagues

Your boss certainly isn't the only one qualified to give you feedback. "The people in the meeting with you or reading your spreadsheets are the ones who actually have the information to help you improve," Heen says. So, when looking for input, don't just look up the organizational chart, but also left, right, and occasionally down. To kickstart a regular feedback loop with colleagues, offer input on, observations about, and praise for their work as well. "You'll get more feedback when you're giving some," says Batista.

Ask more frequently when you're remote

It can be particularly hard to get regular feedback while working remotely since physical distance often prevents informal exchanges. So "the onus is on you" to ask for more input, says Batista. Heen's advice is to "pick up the phone." Don't rely on email or instant messages because nuances tend to get lost.

Adapted from "How to Get the Feedback You Need," on hbr.org, May 15, 2015 (product #H022ZB).

The Family 360 Review

by Scott Edinger

Quick Takes

- Create a safe space
- Give your family the questions in advance
- Tell them what you're hoping to learn
- Listen and ask clarifying questions
- Create a plan to incorporate their feedback

Understanding how others experience us is an important tool for change, in the workplace and especially at home, where it's easy to overlook the impact we have because we are so busy being parents and partners. How can we measure how we're doing as parents? What work tools might we adapt to use at home? Informal 360-degree assessments, which rely on the power of conversation and connection, seem like a good place to start.

I decided to conduct a 360-degree parenting review with my two daughters. When I announced my plans at dinner and said that I needed their help to evaluate my performance as a father, my 9-year-old daughter said, with a fist pump and a giggle, "This is going to be great!" My 16-year-old just said, "Really?!" I reminded them that effective feedback includes pointing out positive behaviors to be reinforced, as well as negative behaviors and areas to improve. My teenager replied, "The negative is going to be a lot easier!"

Both conversations with my daughters were relatively short, between 5 and 10 minutes. My kids were very direct. Most of the feedback they gave was about everyday interactions versus really big issues.

While being a good parent is something I regularly think about and talk about with my family, taking this approach focused the conversation using a process I've worked through with thousands of leaders in my role as a consultant. There are four steps to using a family 360 review to gather meaningful feedback. (This type of review *could* also work with your spouse or partner, but please don't send me the bill for marriage counseling resulting from such an experiment!)

Prepare

To make this a positive experience, give your family member context and a sense of safety.

State your intention and give them questions

Explain that you're looking to improve as a parent and you want their feedback. You may be aware of a specific behavior or pattern of engagement with your child that you want to work on (such as being on your smartphone less or listening before responding with your opinions).

Prepare to ask your child the following three questions:

1. What do I do that you like or that you'd like to see more of?

2. What do I do that you don't like or has a negative impact on you?

3. What would make me a better parent?

Consider giving kids time to think about their answers by sharing the questions in advance.

Set the stage for openness and honesty

Even if you have an open relationship, your kids might be concerned about how you'll receive their feedback. Emphasize that it's OK to share anything—positive or negative. Say something like, "I want to hear your honest opinions. Especially if there's something I do that you don't like, because I really want to understand how my behavior impacts you." Convey that you're strong enough to hear bad news, and that you plan to use their feedback to make important changes in your behavior. Pick a time and place that will make your child feel comfortable; consider asking them to decide where and when you'll talk.

Conduct the Conversation

Begin by again assuring your child that you'll listen with openness and believe what they say. Assure them that their feelings and perspective are valid and prepare to follow through on the safety you've created.

Remind them of your goal and the rules

I told my daughters that I intended to act on what they shared with me, and we could brainstorm ways to implement the changes they were asking for. I asked them to try to be as specific as they could about my behavior.

Ask the three questions

Per her request, my 9-year-old and I sat at our dining room table to talk. She shared this feedback: "Stop correcting me when I'm doing something and let me figure it out, and only help me if I ask for help."

My 16-year-old and I drove to get takeout dinner, and we had our conversation while waiting in the car for our food. She said that she appreciated how I listen to her and give her room to talk in our conversations. But she also shared that sometimes she just doesn't feel like talking.

Listen

Try to listen without judgment to your child's answers. Ask for examples: "Can you tell me about a time when I did that or made you feel that way?" If something is difficult to hear, acknowledge that by saying, "I didn't realize how difficult that's been for you; it's hard for me to hear."

One example my younger daughter shared was a recent bike ride when I had repeatedly told her to stop at a stop sign, increasing my volume to get her attention. It would have been very easy for me to justify myself— that I only correct or help when she needs it, or that I saved her life on that ride. Instead I reflected on her big-picture message—that she hoped to be respected and trusted.

Clarify

Encourage the conversation to go deeper by asking follow-up questions. Your goal is to get a clear and complete understanding of your child's experience.

After my older daughter said she doesn't always feel like talking, I asked, "Can you tell me a little more about that?" She replied, "Not all of our conversations need to be deep, and if something is bothering me, I don't always want to talk about it."

I learned that when she deflects my attempts to have a deeper conversation, I shouldn't get upset with her. Apparently, when we've had these interactions in the past, I've seemed disappointed, which made her feel bad.

Manage your emotions

This entire process will backfire if you don't respond with grace and appreciation. If you don't like the feedback you receive, remind yourself that your goal is to understand your child's perspective. If you get angry or upset, you can seriously harm the relationship you're trying to improve. So, take a breath and try to maintain your curiosity.

Respond

When it's your turn to talk, be calm and open, always mindful that they're taking a risk in sharing information that may upset you. Avoid asking questions in a way that feels like an interrogation. Softness in language and facial expressions help when you say things like, "Can you help me understand how I did that?" When my teen said she appreciated that I always allowed her to share her point of view, I acknowledged that I've always felt it was important for her to have a strong voice and assured her that I would continue to do this.

Thank them

No matter how you feel about their feedback, remember that your child took the time to do what you asked, so acknowledge their cooperation and say thank you.

Summarize what you heard

Review and acknowledge the primary messages you've received. For my 9-year-old, I said that I heard that she wanted me to let her figure things out for herself. For my teenager, I said that I heard her say that, while she appreciated my willingness to listen to her point of view, not every conversation had to be deep and meaningful.

Follow Up

Now you're ready to develop a plan for change. Based on the feedback you've received, you'll probably have some ideas about what you can do differently. Just like leadership development plans, a family plan that focuses on grand actions once a month will not be effective. To produce real change, come up with a few ideas you can do every day, even multiple times per day.

Reflect on what you heard

Reflect on what your family member has shared and look for themes. I began to see a pattern in my own behavior as both my daughters shared feedback about getting out of their way: I recognized I need to let my kids grow up. My 9-year-old's request to figure things out for herself rang true for me. I was both proud of her for expressing her independence and a little sheepish because I realized she was right.

You might be surprised to find that something you've been doing that you meant to be positive had unintended negative consequences. Like my attempts to engage my teenager in meaningful conversation. I learned that the way *she* wanted to connect wasn't always what I had in mind. At the end of our chat, I confirmed my understanding that not all conversations need to be deep, and if she wants to talk about something light, like a TV show or silly memes, I could accept that as an equally important way to connect.

Brainstorm ideas

Share the information from these conversations with your spouse or partner and brainstorm ideas for change. Once you have some ideas in mind, share them with your child and talk about what you might do differently.

You can say: "Thanks again for being willing to talk with me. I've been thinking about the feedback you shared, and I want to tell you what I plan to start doing differently." Just two or three meaningful things that you plan to work on will make all the difference.

I told my 9-year-old, "I'm going to try to do more of the things you enjoy, like taking time out of my workday to play a game and have fun with you. I'm also going to work on letting you figure things out. Especially when you probably know what to do without me." You could also discuss ways your child might gently remind you when they see you falling into old habits, such as creating a code word or signal they could use.

Keep the conversation going

Tell your family member that they can talk with you about how your behavior impacts them at any time, with the expectation that you will listen and respond. Let them know that this initial conversation was a great start, and that you hope it'll continue over time. Consider ways to have regular feedback conversations, either as needed or by scheduling them around a milestone such as a birthday.

• • •

One of the best things to come out of this experience was hearing my teen say that she felt I was in the top 1% of dads just for asking her these questions and not pushing back on her feedback. I have no idea if I'm in the top 1% of dads, and it really doesn't matter. What does matter is that I gave my daughter a chance to express her perspective on my parenting, I took her concerns seriously, and I responded nondefensively. And that may be one of the most valuable lessons of all for a parent.

Adapted from "Learn to Solicit Feedback . . . from Your Kids," on hbr.org, July 17, 2020 (product #H05PBY).

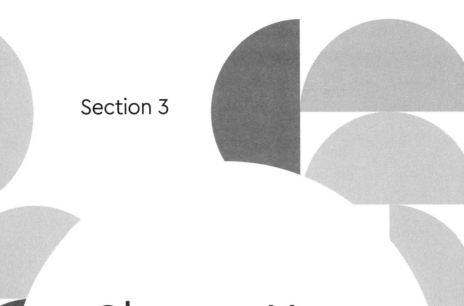

Section 3

Choose Your Own Adventure

Set Goals and Make Career Choices

Increase the Odds of Achieving Your Goals by Setting Them with Your Family

by Jackie Coleman and John Coleman

Quick Takes

- Establish an annual meeting to set goals
- Identify family, couple, and individual goals (even for kids)
- Use a set of questions to structure the conversation
- Hold each other accountable and share constructive feedback
- Check in on each other's progress

"Work" and "life" come up in our thoughts and conversation as separate and, all too often, in tension. We make annual resolutions, detailed daily plans, and to-do lists, but we do so as individuals, generally not sharing those plans or planning jointly with those closest to us. And we often think of our personal and professional goals as occupying distinct and separate spheres. But what if the work and home spheres could merge and actually improve the odds that we'll meet our goals?

Research shows that it's easier to achieve our goals when we're not trying to go it alone. One study found a positive correlation between participation in digital communities and reaching fitness goals.[1] Similarly, a study of rowers found that training together heightened their threshold for pain.[2]

For many of us, our closest and most trusted companion is a spouse. Couples in committed, long-term relationships often make plans to manage busy days or take fun trips, but rarely set resolutions or actively create long-term plans together. By not doing so, couples may actually be making it harder to achieve their goals. We decided to experiment with fully integrating our personal planning for the year. We've always informally mentioned our goals to each other, but this time around, we talked with intentionality about why we were chasing those goals, and how we planned to get there. By including each other in the process, we invited the other not only to be aware of what we plan to accomplish, but also to hold us accountable as we strive to reach these goals.

If you don't have a spouse or partner, you can still try these techniques with a family member, trusted colleague, close friend, or other ally. And parents might even think about including kids in some or all of these meetings to take advantage of their creativity and to help them focus and build life skills.

Our experience, combined with research we've evaluated and other couples we've consulted with, led to the following tips for effective planning within the context of a family.

Hold an Annual Board Meeting

Several years ago, we attended a seminar where speakers Rick and Jill Woolworth introduced the idea of an "annual meeting" for families—taking time at the end of each year to evaluate that year and plan for the next. Establishing this as a norm assures that goal setting happens on a set schedule rather than haphazardly or in isolation. For us, this happened over the holidays between Christmas and the new year, and included a discussion of the past year, how we performed against our goals, and how we felt about life as a couple, as individuals, and as a family as a whole. We wrote out our specific goals for the year and the habits we hoped to develop. Then we discussed them and how each of us could help the other achieve our goals. These annual meetings provide accountability, but more important, establish a vision for the year ahead. Then, as so many have advised, break these annual goals down into habits, monthly and weekly goals, and daily to-dos.[3]

By talking about your goals with your spouse or other allies and writing them down, you've already improved your odds of success. In *Yes!: 50 Scientifically Proven Ways to Be Persuasive*, authors Noah Goldstein, Steve Martin, and Robert Cialdini explain how making an active commitment directly affects action.[4] In one of the studies they reference, researchers found that out of a group of individuals who passively agreed to participate in a volunteer project, only 17% showed up to participate. Contrast that with those who agreed to volunteer through active means (writing it down, signing a contract, and so forth), 49% appeared as promised. Writing down specific goals and sharing them with your family is like signing a contract. It not only increases social accountability but also allows your spouse and others to think about specific ways in which they can support you in achieving your goals.

Set Joint Goals

The second essential component of annual planning is setting joint goals. What do you hope to achieve as a family? As a couple? As individuals (including your children)? What habits do you hope to develop together? Work-life balance is often cited as a key factor in job satisfaction, yet many of us struggle to achieve it. The people with whom you share your life are likely the best people to help you plan for balancing it. And joint goals can assure that your personal and professional pursuits are more fully aligned.

Hold Each Other Accountable

Once you've made your plans, help hold each other accountable. When you invite someone to join you in setting and striving for goals, you're not only asking them to cheer you on when you reach certain landmarks, you're also empowering them to point out when you're unfocused or offtrack. This requires recognizing that constructive feedback can be hard to hear and letting go of some ego and pride. To make the process easier and give your partner permission to hold you accountable, use a structured set of questions:

- What are 2–3 areas in which I'm falling short of my goals?

- What are 2–3 areas in which I'm succeeding?

- What's 1 thing I can do to improve this month?

Specifically working through questions like these helps focus the conversation and keep a balance between negative and positive feedback.

Check Your Progress

At the end of each month, check in on your progress using structured questions that work for your family. While making plans as a family is a good start, it's not enough to make things happen. Allow yourself regular checkpoints throughout the year to see where you are in developing habits and reaching your goals. Make it fun and something to look forward to. Order takeout or have a special meal. Keep the focus of the conversation on celebrating progress and identifying the setbacks of the month. Consider how you might build on things that are going well and brainstorm ways to get back on track when a goal or habit is off course. Some couples might be tempted to do this weekly, but monthly feedback seems to be the most realistic time frame. Once a month is enough time for you to have made meaningful progress but also frequent enough to allow you to course correct throughout the year.

• • •

Planning for both professional and personal goals with your spouse or other trusted ally can help you better care for one another, ensure that you're focused on the issues that matter most in the context of your family, enlist your biggest supporters in helping you achieve your goals and get things done, and teach your children about communication and partnership.

Adapted from "Increase the Odds of Achieving Your Goals by Setting Them with Your Spouse," on hbr.org, February 3, 2015 (product #H01UL0).

Flex Work, Part-Time, and Laterals, Oh My!

by Michele Benton

Quick Takes

- Identify the types of arrangements your company uses
- Emphasize your impact, not your hours
- Pause before you say yes to extra work
- Consider assignments that provide visibility and opportunity to learn
- Clarify how responsibilities at home might shift

Before having kids, we envision ourselves as the devoted company worker, always present, fully committed, and willing to give extra effort to get the job done. But with kids come new demands, especially for the majority of us who are in dual-career households.[1] Our commitment and career ambitions hold true; it's just harder to fit life around traditional work structures. It would seem that alternative work programs—flexible hours, remote work, part-time salaried work, job shares, and lateral moves—create a win-win for employers, employees, and families.

Unfortunately, alternative work is a bit of a ruse. Most employers offer it,[1] usually as part of their inclusion programs to attract quality talent (you). But, often it's an empty gesture, as few employees ever use these options.[2] Research in the United States and Europe confirms consequences[2] we already know: Using these programs means certain career death.[3]

We desperately need these options. Not on paper, but in practice in our lives. With no yellow brick road to follow, we must find our own way forward. Here are four steps to making an alternative work program work for you.

Get Real

Just because a company is recognized as a top employer for parents doesn't mean alternative work is mainstream.[4] Often, it functions like a glorified mommy track, and access is based on manager preference (and what works in one department may not work in yours). In developing your alternative work proposal, look around, chat with colleagues, and tap into HR to assess potential acceptance and barriers:

- Do senior leaders "get it"? How many are parents of young children or part of a dual-career couple? What unstated messages do they send about family and work?

- What types of alternative work are accepted? Is it only "work from home Fridays" or are other types commonplace? Which department or roles permit it? Are certain managers more accepting?

- What happens to people who use alternative work? How do they get big projects or promotions? Do they have a senior-level sponsor, a plan to ramp back up, or something else for support?

Make It Worthwhile

Build on areas of acceptance and overcome barriers by helping your leaders realize there are different ways to show career commitment:

- **Craft a value proposition.** Assess what impact you have on revenue, profit, efficiency, or costs, and connect it to your proposal. For example, your part-time role saves $1 million in outside vendor fees, working "three days" remotely delivers $300,000 in sales, or a lateral move closes a gap without the costs or downtime of a temp. Be creative—for ideas, tap a finance friend.

- **Talk about outcomes, not hours.** Many cultures tend to focus on busyness, time, or effort when discussing work. Instead, highlight your efficient method, innovative use of resources, or creative thinking skills. (Think of yourself as a consultant who charges by project deliverable, not billable hours.) During performance reviews, champion your accomplishments and make the case for a meaningful salary increase and bonus. Steer conversations toward your bottom-line value.

- **Protect what you hope to gain.** If your goal is fewer hours, don't automatically work longer than agreed or overcompensate in an exhaustive frenzy while at work. If you want less intensity in your lateral position, make sure an additional project brings promotable skills or senior stakeholder visibility before you take it on. Be selective when giving discretionary effort.

- **Make it normal.** Avoid signaling that alternative work is wrong. You wouldn't apologize to colleagues if you weren't available one evening or on a Sunday morning, so don't apologize for not working conventional hours. Simply state what's possible: *I'm not available Monday, but I'm open 9–2 Tuesday.* Or, *I can have it ready Friday; would that work?* Choose words that reinforce professionalism, such as *work remotely* (vs. *work from home*), or *I'm in transit* (vs. *I'm in my car*).

- **Push for career support.** Seek senior-level mentors and talk up how your alternative work arrangement is creating results. Before talent discussions, check in with your manager to prepare them to advocate for you. Let decision makers know you're interested in high-potential leadership training and resources.

Buck Gender Assumptions

Even though family structures have evolved into count-less variations, stereotypes of life divided between a working husband and a stay-at-home wife linger.[5] With alternative work programs, men get the benefit of the doubt while women get punished as motherhood seems incompatible with work commitment.[6] At home, alternative work for women usually translates into more domestic burden, like childcare or housework, but for most men, it facilitates other work arenas like training or a side gig.[7] Consider how gender assumptions intersect with the life you're trying to create:

- When changing job structure, be clear about what things you're taking on outside work. Make sure you and your partner feel expectations and trade-offs are fair, and frame shared duties the same way (is it parenting or babysitting?).

- A lot of advice today encourages women to recast their definition of success away from power and money to things like well-being or family satisfaction, and to be at peace with dropping the ball or opting out.[8] Define success for yourself.

Vote with Your Feet

Finally, if you can't get support for an alternative program that works for you, take your talent elsewhere. Reallocate discretionary time to job searching. In your exit interview, tell HR exactly why you're leaving, because company execs read these reports.

When it comes to creating career opportunities that support your life and goals outside of work, your words and actions can help transform alternative work from good policy to good practice.

Adapted from "Adventures in Alternative Work Arrangements," on hbr.org, July 7, 2020 (product #H05PCB).

Winning Support for Flexible Work

by Amy Gallo

Quick Takes

- Ask yourself what you want to accomplish
- Propose it as an experiment
- Consult with your team
- Highlight professional impact

Many working parents seek flexible work arrangements to accommodate lives that don't mesh with being present in an office on a traditional schedule, five days a week. And research from Lotte Bailyn, MIT management professor and coauthor of *Beyond Work-Family Balance*, shows that when employees have the flexibility they need, they meet goals more easily, they're absent or tardy less often, and their morale goes up. Yet not every company has an official policy or program for alternative arrangements—and not every manager is willing or equipped to provide them for members of their teams. This doesn't mean you should give up on the idea of flextime if it would help you feel less harried, cut down a lengthy commute, be more present with your kids, or avoid burnout. It just means that the onus is on you to propose a plan that works for you, your boss, and your company. By focusing your proposal on the benefits research has shown and thoughtfully framing your request around them, you greatly increase your chances of getting approval for an alternative work arrangement.

Define What You Want

The first step is to figure out what you're trying to accomplish. Is your goal to spend more time with family? Less time at the office? Or do you want to remove distractions so that you can focus on bigger, longer-term projects? Once you're clear on your goal, decide how you can achieve it while still doing your job effectively. Options include having a compressed workweek, job sharing, working remotely, and taking a sabbatical. Of course, not every job is suited for a flexible arrangement. Before you make a proposal, think about the impact your wished-for scenario will have on your boss, your team, and your performance.

Next, investigate what policies, if any, your company has and whether there's a precedent for flexibility. You won't need to blaze a trail if one already exists.

Design It as an Experiment

Some managers will hesitate to approve a flexible work arrangement, especially if your organization lacks established protocols. Allay their fears by positioning your proposal as an experiment. "Include a trial period so your boss doesn't worry that things will fall apart," says Bailyn. "He or she needs to be able to see the new way of working."

In his book *Total Leadership: Be a Better Leader, Have a Richer Life*, Stewart D. Friedman talks about nine types of experiments you can do to gently introduce flexibility—everything from working remotely to delegating. Whatever you propose, provide an out. Explain that if it doesn't work, you're willing to try a different arrangement or resume your former routine. "One can always go back to the original plan, but most such experiments work out very well," says Bailyn.

Ask for Team Input

"Our research has shown that flexibility only works when it's done collectively, not one-on-one between employee and employer," says Bailyn. Your team is affected by your work schedule, so you need everyone's support to make your new arrangement a success. Explain what you're trying to achieve and ask for their input. "Engage them in the planning," Bailyn says, and let your boss know that you've incorporated your colleagues' suggestions into your proposal.

Involving your team can help head off another common concern: Some bosses worry that if they grant one person flexibility, the floodgates will open and everyone will want the same arrangement. This is often an unfounded fear. Friedman points out that there's a difference between *equality* and *equity*, and, in fact, many people prefer a traditional schedule. "You don't give everyone the same thing because they don't *want* the same thing," he says.

Highlight the Benefits to the Organization

Emphasize the organizational benefits over the personal ones. "Whatever you try has to be designed very consciously to not just be about you or your family," Friedman says. "Instead, have the clear goal of improving your performance at work and making your boss successful." Demonstrate that you have considered the company's needs, that your new arrangement will not be disruptive, and that it will actually have positive benefits, such as improving your productivity or increasing your relevant knowledge.

Reassess and Make Adjustments

Once your flexible work arrangement has been in place for three or four months, evaluate its success. Are you reaching your goals? Is the arrangement causing problems for anyone? Because you've designed it as a trial, you'll want to report back to your boss. "Get the data to support your productivity. Show that it's working," says Friedman. And if it's not, be prepared to suggest changes.

Adapted from content posted on hbr.org, December 1, 2010 (product #H006JJ).

Make Part-Time Work for You

An Interview with Kristin McElderry by Amy Gallo

Quick Takes

- Be intentional about where your team is located
- Share your career goals with your boss
- Evaluate and adjust your allocations
- Establish communication norms with your team

We spoke with Kristin McElderry, an incredibly organized consultant and mother of three, whose part-time schedule hasn't kept her from getting promoted. We talked about what it's been like working three days a week for a large professional services firm. Working part-time as a manager, especially in consulting, where people often put in long hours and are on call for clients, is pretty unusual. And she says that while her role is complicated and not typical, her career is going pretty well.

AMY GALLO: *How long have you been working part-time?*

KRISTIN McELDERRY: I've worked part-time for the last five years. But within that span, I've taken two maternity leaves, which were almost a year each, so about three years. I just came back from my third maternity leave; this was my first full week back. So, I'm definitely in a transition state right now.

AG: *What made you want to work part-time?*

KM: After I had my first child, I was on the fence about going back to work at all. A lot of my friends are stay-at-home moms, and I had considered it. Many work part-time, but in more traditional part-time roles, like nursing, something with just a couple shifts a week or every few weeks. In my field, it's not very common to work part-time. But a leader from my project team reached out and said, "Hey, I've got this. I know you've been on the fence. I think you could do it part-time. Would you consider it?" So I had a meeting, and I brought the baby with me. We talked about what part-time might look like, and I came back.

They said, "You tell me how many days you need." At my firm, you just take a percentage—you do 40%, 60%, 80%, whatever you need. I wrote the terms, and they signed them.

AG: *There wasn't much of a negotiation?*

KM: Not really. They came to me with the role. My skills were in demand, which was a great position for me to be in. So, I was able to set the terms. I recognize a lot of people don't have that opportunity.

I was very intentional about working in Massachusetts. In my firm, you can work all over the country. And prior to starting to work exclusively in Massachusetts, I was on an airplane Monday through Thursday. I was very intentional about trying to get involved with a local account team so that I would be doing local work. That's what enabled me to continue doing what I do, because if I were being asked to do full-time travel for work right now, I would say no.

One thing that's challenging about part-time is if you want to transition to another firm, it is hard. I get approached by headhunters and recruiters fairly often. And I always say, "OK, I work part-time. You have an 80% travel clause. I'm not really willing to do that." And that abruptly halts the conversation.

AG: *Were you worried about your career and the implications of being part-time?*

KM: Definitely. I've had many conversations when I've been concerned about what that means, including a really interesting conversation with my boss. I'd been back on an account after a leave with my second child, and I thought I was doing good work. But my confidence in being able to get promoted to the next level while part-time was low. In my firm, you do your project work, but a lot of what helps you get to that next level is extra stuff. It's contributing to the firm, taking on what we call "plus ones." And I felt like my plus one was doing a full-time job in three days. I didn't really feel I was going to be able to do anything else. I was at my limit. So, I had a pretty frank conversation with my boss. He said, "You want to make senior manager this year?" I said, "Yeah, I do." And he said, "OK, let's make it happen. I think you're on the track; I think you're doing the things you need to do." I did make senior manager this year, while I was on leave. This is my second time getting promoted while on maternity leave. I've definitely felt supported. So I'm working with the same team again. And it's tough. I feel like moving to the next level—I don't know for sure how that's going to happen. It's a much bigger jump. I'd be moving into a managing director or partner role. And I don't see a lot of people doing that part-time.

AG: *How have your peers felt about you working part-time?*

KM: They've been primarily supportive. It's tricky sometimes just because of scheduling constraints. There haven't been specific challenges, but I've never felt specifically targeted. I've been able to pull my full-time weight in three days. If I wasn't, maybe there'd be a little bit more conflict.

AG: *How do you do a full-time job in three days?*

KM: I'm highly efficient with my time. It's getting trickier, especially now that I have three kids and it's harder to even go out in the morning. I feel I've already lived a full day before the day's started! I was highly efficient with my time, but I also wasn't doing a lot of those extra things I mentioned. Where before I might've had bandwidth to do those extra things, now I'm getting my job done and calling it a day.

AG: *A lot of the advice given to women who are considering going part-time is, "Don't do it. You're going to get paid half the amount or 60% of the amount, and you're still going to do a full-time job." Do you feel like that's been the case for you?*

KM: I got the same advice from one of my main mentors. She said, "Everybody I know who works part-time works more." And I definitely can see how that can happen. Before when I returned from leave, I really eased into it. This time, it's been a little quicker. I've gotten dropped into some pretty challenging work very quickly. And I'm probably going to up my allocation a bit because it's going to be tricky to do what I need to do. But I've advanced, so there's more expected. I definitely think working part-time makes sense for certain roles and doesn't make sense for other roles. And it is more challenging as you get more senior.

AG: *Tell me why.*

KM: Because you manage more people. In one of my last roles, I was managing 10 or 11 folks. They were all pretty junior, a year or two out of college. They all worked five days, and I was working three days. Giving them the mentorship, coaching, and feedback that they needed was tricky to do in three days, in addition to client meetings and everything else. So how many hours a day you have and managing a big team is really challenging. The scope of what you do gets bigger. One of the things that'll be tricky for me in the next few years is that I'm involved in a lot more work where we're responding to requests for proposals, and we're writing proposals that are very time sensitive. Sometimes people ask us for a proposal in a week. And it doesn't matter what days of the week I have childcare lined up. If the proposal is due Friday, it's due Friday. And that makes it trickier.

AG: *Do you find yourself working a lot on days you're not supposed to be working?*

KM: No. I may take a phone call here and there or a text message because that's the norm I established with my team. I did have some experiences where I would totally sign off, and then work wouldn't continue. Then I'd get back and they'd say, "Oh well, I didn't know what to do, so I just stopped." I said, "Me working part-time is not an excuse for you not to do your job. If you're stuck, text me."

AG: *Do you communicate pretty regularly with the team you're working with about your hours and your boundaries?*

KM: I've definitely had to do that. They'll set something up, and I'll say, "I'm not able to attend. Let me send somebody because I won't be there." My boss asked me for something yesterday and I said, "Frankly, I don't have time—I don't have the bandwidth today." I was teetering, thinking, Should I send this? Should I not send this? Then I thought, I have to.

AG: *Do you have any concern that setting boundaries around your availability will impact your career or people's impression of you?*

KM: Sometimes. Deciding to be part-time is making a decision about your career in some ways. If I was trying to be the CEO or make partner next year, I wouldn't choose to be part-time. I am consciously choosing to opt out in some ways just because I'm not willing to give work 100% of my 40 hours a week right now.

AG: *Do you think you'll be part-time forever?*

KMY: For a while, given the demands in our family. We're trying out an au pair. I'm hoping that makes some things flexible. I'm hoping to move up to four days. But with the ages of my children—and my husband has a fantastic and demanding career as well—it's just not going to be feasible for me to go full-time. There's going to be a point when I'm going to want to ramp up my career advancement. But this just isn't that phase right now.

Adapted from "How to Make Part-Time Work for You," on Women at Work *(podcast), November 18, 2019.*

How to Decide Whether to Relocate for a Job

by Rebecca Knight

Quick Takes

- Ask, Who do I want to become?
- Propose a temporary stint to test out the new location
- Consider the long-term impact on you and your family
- Find out what your next move would be
- Solicit advice from trusted peers

Sometimes the perfect job isn't down the street, but rather thousands of miles—or perhaps even an ocean—away. If you're offered a job in a different location, how do you know if it's worth relocating? Who should help you make the decision? And, how do you weigh the potential upsides like money and opportunity against costs like the impact on your family or the loss of your existing network?

What the Experts Say

Whether or not to relocate for a new role is a big decision both professionally and personally. "There are so many factors to consider," says Jennifer Petriglieri, an associate professor at INSEAD and author of *Couples That Work: How Dual-Career Couples Can Thrive in Love and Work.* "What's the opportunity? What's the longevity [of the job]? And what's the family situation?" Indeed, the decision is especially complicated if you have a partner and children, says Matthew Bidwell, an associate professor at Wharton whose research focuses on patterns of work and employment. "It's not just, what does this mean for *your* career, but what does this mean for *our* family?" he says. Relocating for a job can often be "great for your personal and professional development," but it's also "a risk and a leap into the unknown." Here are some ideas to help you think through whether the move is right for you.

Think holistically

When you're wrestling with a big decision, "there's a temptation to get out an Excel spreadsheet and weigh the pros and cons," says Petriglieri. But this is an instance where Excel comes up short. "When you're choosing one life over another, it becomes an identity choice: Who do I want to become? What kind of family will we be?" The job is only one piece of the puzzle. Consider your "holistic happiness and satisfaction." Think about the lifestyle that the new location affords or lacks. Are you suited for small-town life? Or do you prefer a big city? Do you want to spend your weekends traveling? Or do you want to feel rooted in a community? The answers to these questions will help you uncover what this "move means for you, your partner, and your children," she says. "When it's a difficult choice, it means that no option is clearly better than the other." Try to think beyond the immediate move, suggests Bidwell. "Ask, What is best for us in the long-term?"

Talk through the move with your partner a lot . . .

The most important person in this equation is your partner, says Bidwell. "The big issue is what does this move do to your partner's career?" Will they be able to find meaningful work in the new place? If not, how big of a setback will it be? "There's quite a lot of research showing that people suffer from putting their career on hold," he says. If your partner won't have a job in the new location, "the move brings up other issues because you're taking them away from their support network." He points to a certain unhappiness known as trailing spouse syndrome. "You have a new job, new office, and all sorts of new people to meet; your spouse has been dropped in the middle of nowhere and knows no one." Petriglieri notes that trailing spouses often bear the brunt of move-related household tasks. "It's tough," she says. "Whenever you move, for the first six months, you are in the trenches." And it takes a huge toll. "Research on why relocations fail always points to the unhappiness of the trailing spouse," she says.[1]

. . . And talk to your kids a little

"It's possible to move at any time with kids, but certain ages are more difficult than others," says Petriglieri. Many people, for instance, are reluctant to move when their kids are teenagers; when kids are younger than eight, the prospect of uprooting them is much less daunting. Petriglieri says that while obviously you need to speak with your children about a potential move, she cautions, "there is a danger of consulting them too much because it brings up a lot of anxiety unnecessarily." Children, she says, "have a harder time imagining what their life will be like" in a new place. They might become resistant to move, which will make things much harder on you. Bidwell concurs: "The kids may complain, but they will adjust." Keep your eyes on the prize. The relocation "is a potentially enriching and stimulating experience."

Consider your development

Moving to a new job in a new city is a surefire way to help "round out" your skills and experience, says Bidwell. "You'll get to know people from different parts of the company; you'll be exposed to new ideas; you'll be able to build a broader network." And if you're relocating overseas, you'll gain an "understanding of a different culture." Indeed, in many organizations, "some form of international experience is necessary to get that top job." But recognize that the relocation poses "long- and short-term trade-offs" to your development. For instance, "the new cultural context you're learning comes at the expense of your loss of network back home." To keep that from happening, "make sure you're on the radar screen" with your home office "having conversations with all the right people on a regular basis," Bidwell says.

Find out what's next . . .

You must also think about the opportunity within the context of your long-term professional path. "Most companies are not likely to offer you a relocation unless there's something pretty big in it for you, meaning a significant promotion and raise," Petriglieri says. But the question you need to ask is, "What's the next move after this?" If, say, you're an American considering a three-year stint in London or Paris, that question is less complicated. "It's a no-brainer that you will probably return to the U.S." But if you're asked to "head up operations in Denver or Cleveland," the calculation is a little trickier. And yet, while it's important to think about next steps, you need to have reasonable expectations, says Bidwell. "There is a tension there," he says. "On one hand you want to have a conversation about where do I go after this? But realistically, the company can't give you a definitive answer." And besides, "career paths tend to be haphazard for most of us."

. . . And whether there's an escape hatch

Worst-case scenario: You and your family are miserable. What then? "You need to think about an escape hatch if you don't like it or if it doesn't gel for your family," says Petriglieri. It somewhat depends on the location itself. "When you are relocating to a hub city and it doesn't work out, there are often other options, but if you're moving somewhere more isolated, it's harder." The specifics of the role you're considering are also key. Make sure you're not professionally pigeonholing yourself "by taking on a specialist role," she says. Another danger, says Bidwell, is "staying too long" in your adopted city. "There's a risk that if you stay in a role for a long time, you become a specialist for that region," he says. This is why he recommends "talking with your partner beforehand about how long you're going for and agree on an exit plan."

Seek advice

It's often helpful to solicit input from others—with one caveat. "You want to talk with people who are not too close to the issue," says Petriglieri. Your boss, for instance, may try to convince you to go. After all, there's presumably "a business need" and a reason you've been asked to move in the first place. And friends and family members have a vested interest in your choice. "No one is neutral, and these conversations can become charged." Ideally, she says, you should talk with "a group of trusted peers" who "have similar family issues and similar career aspirations." These people can be "a good sounding board" as you evaluate your options. Bidwell agrees. He suggests seeking advice from colleagues who've done similar stints as well as others in your industry. "You need moderately unbiased views of what to expect."

Request a tryout

If you're uncertain, it may be worth asking your organization if you could do a temporary stint or job swap in the proposed location before making a big move, says Petriglieri. "Relocations are extremely costly," she says. "Failed relocations are even worse." She says companies are "increasingly willing to allow employees to do short-term relocations or secondments" to maximize the likelihood of success. In essence, your employer would be giving you a chance "to try before you buy." Even if your organization does not offer this opportunity, "you can always ask," says Bidwell.

Don't overanalyze

Whether or not to relocate is a big decision—but beware of analysis paralysis, overthinking a situation so that a decision is never made, or one is made by default. Try to have perspective. "As you get older, there are very few decisions in life where you don't feel some ambivalence," says Petriglieri. "A career is long," she adds. "We can all afford a few adventures, and we have plenty of time to experiment and explore." However, don't assume that this is your one chance at trying something new. If you're miserable, you can course correct, says Bidwell. "You have to take risks in your career," he says. "Sometimes it doesn't work out, and so, you figure out what to do next."

Case Study: Consider the Next Phase of Your Career

Anne Chow spent the first 15 years of her career at AT&T, earning promotion after promotion, at the company's headquarters in New Jersey. "It was very easy to move around the company without geographically moving my family," she says.

In 2005, after AT&T was purchased by SBC, Anne was asked to move to Texas, where the new company was based. At the time, Anne had young children, and she was reluctant to move away from her parents. She was also hesitant about Texas itself. "I am a Jersey Girl and East Coast through and through," she says.

She declined to move. But by 2014, her perspective had changed. Her career was going well; her kids were older—middle school and high school; and her husband was retired. "I was questioning what I wanted to do next and what I wanted the next phase of my career to look like," she says.

She briefly considered outside opportunities, but after 24 years at AT&T, she wanted to "double-down on [her] commitment to the company." She broached the topic of moving with her family. "My husband was supportive, and my children were in," she recalls. "I declared myself mobile to move to Texas."

Shortly thereafter, the CEO tapped her to take on a new job leading sales operations and solutions. Once the relocation became real, her children changed their minds. "When we told the kids, they said we should go without them," she says.

She and her family had many long talks. "We talked about who we wanted to be," she says. "My husband had 51% of the vote. I was worried about his social infrastructure because it was his life that would change the most. The kids would assimilate."

After three years in Dallas, Anne has already had three different positions. Today she is the president of the national business.

Despite her career success, she admits that the first year was difficult for her spouse and kids. "It definitely made us a stronger family," she says. "But I don't know if we'll ever call it home."

Adapted from content posted on hbr.org, December 3, 2018 (product #H04OBG).

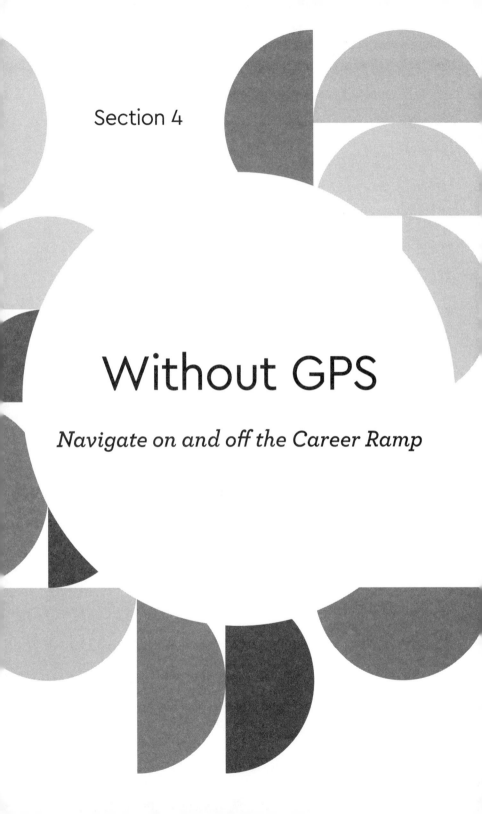

Section 4

Without GPS

Navigate on and off the Career Ramp

When You're Leaving Your Job Because of Your Kids

by Daisy Dowling

Quick Takes

- Lead with the important info and be neutral when you quit

- Prepare responses for negative reactions

- Remain open to new roles or career opportunities

- Coach your colleagues through your departure

- Take your relationships with you

You've decided to leave your organization, and the decision was driven by your needs as a working parent. Maybe you're taking a new job with fewer hours or less travel so that you can spend more time with the kids; maybe you're "up-ramping" and taking on a position with more responsibility, pressure, and pay so that you can afford those looming college bills; or maybe you've decided to focus on responsibilities at home before looking for a different opportunity.

Regardless of the specific reason why, the question now is how—how to leave in the right way, how to be credible, honest, and transparent while acting in your own best interests, and how to preserve the long-term career capital you've worked so hard to create.

Unfortunately for working parents, there's no off-boarding playbook, and when you've got your kids and family in mind, the raft of emotions attached to a professional exit can swell to very large proportions. You may feel guilty, excited, conflicted, angry, or relieved, perhaps all at the same time, none of which puts you on your front foot to handle your exit in a way that can enhance your network or career.

But there are strategies that work—specific techniques that can make your transition as effective and nonstressful as possible.

As a longtime HR professional, I watched many employees make career changes, some very effectively and gracefully, and learned their personal techniques and approaches. Now, as an executive coach and adviser to working-parent professionals, I work with many people looking to make career transitions and advise them on incorporating these strategies in their moves. And as a full-time working mother who's changed jobs twice since my first daughter arrived, I've had the chance to use them myself.

Here are seven tactics any working parent should use when transitioning out of a job.

Say it plain—without an edge

"Bill, I've decided to leave the organization. I've taken a role at Other Company that will give me the flexibility to meet my family responsibilities in the way I need to." Like a good newspaper article, the most important information should be conveyed up front, factually, and neutrally. Don't wait five minutes into the conversation to make your announcement, and don't address any gripes you had about the lifestyle or hours on the job when breaking the news—keep those in the rearview mirror.

Be a class act—regardless of your feelings

Even if your manager screamed at you about missing a weekly update meeting to take your sick child to the pediatrician, it's time to rise above. Remember: Last impressions are lasting impressions, and yours need to convey your value and style as a professional. Saying "I've appreciated the four years I spent here, and the opportunity to be part of a great team" puts you in a much better long-term position than a negative statement will.

Play through the negative reaction

Your manager may be surprised, or even angry. Maybe you were the "work-life poster child" the company wanted to keep, or maybe your departure means the department loses head count. Prepare for negative reactions—pushback, derision, irritation, disbelief—and rehearse the jujitsu moves you can make to neutralize them. Empathize and acknowledge: "I understand this is a surprise." Make things more personal: "I understand your point of view as a leader of the company, but I've made this decision as an individual, and a father." And praise: "My decision has nothing to do with how I see you as a manager. You've been a great advocate for me, and I appreciate it."

Keep an open mind

Many of my working-parent coachees are shocked, upon resigning, to find out how much their organizations value them—and are suddenly willing to provide new roles, more flexibility, even sabbatical leaves in a desperate bid to keep them. As firm as your intention to leave is, remain open to new options that are offered. You may find an unexpected solution that's actually better than the one you've committed to. At the very least, it's worth a conversation.

Put on blinders

Inevitably, any working parent leaving their job for anything remotely to do with family reasons will be on the receiving end of editorial comments—lots and lots of them, some clumsy ("Couldn't take it, huh?") to well intentioned but disheartening ("Be careful—my law school roommate left after her first was born and she could never find a job again"). The comments have nothing to do with you, so ignore them. Put on blinders, look down the straightaway, and run your own race, with the guardrails and mile markers you've set for yourself—not the ones others set for you.

Become a consultant

Once the announcement has been made, go above and beyond to help your colleagues transition into their future without you. Spreadsheet summaries, checklists, flowcharts documenting complex operations, project planning meetings—pretend you're from McKinsey, and your job is to help the organization manage without you. Stay late a few days to demonstrate how committed you are to supporting colleagues through your departure. You'll look like the top-flight professional you are—efficient, professional, and graceful to boot.

Take your relationships with you

When you leave a job, don't leave your professional connections along with it. Take the relationships you've had—with managers, colleagues, mentors, mentees, and everyone in between—into your next role, even if your next role is spending time at home. Statements like "While we won't be working together anymore, I want you to know that I've always considered you a mentor, and will continue to" or "I certainly hope we get to be members of the same team again" appeal to and leave lasting positive impressions with the crustiest of colleagues. Think of your professional network as a portfolio, and make sure that no important assets fall out of it as you change roles.

Anyone making a working-parent-related job change will inevitably have some concerns and self-doubt. But by focusing on the mechanics of your exit, you can make the transition resound to your credit and keep doors open for the future.

Adapted from content posted on hbr.org, April 11, 2017 (product # H03LD7).

Ramp Up Your Career After Parental Leave

by Lisa Quest

Quick Takes

- Identify your career goals
- Cut out tasks and meetings that don't advance your goal
- Focus on what you can do in the time you have
- Conduct regular conversations at work and at home
- Reassess your goals and adjust course
- Pay it forward

Returning from parental leave can be a jarring inflection point that too often results in people curtailing their responsibilities or leaving their jobs altogether. While many women choose to return to work after maternity leave, many others find that it's not sustainable and leave or take on reduced roles. Seventeen percent of women and 4% of men stop working in the five years following childbirth, according to research recently conducted at the Universities of Bristol and Essex in the United Kingdom.[1] Harvard economist Claudia Goldin has found that the gender wage gap in America is the largest for women in their prime childbearing years.[2]

Navigating a system that was not designed for career paths that balance work with family can easily feel like a mission-practically-impossible even in the best of times. And when the job market is weak, many people will become even more pessimistic about the possibility of persuading an employer to accept a flexible work arrangement.

After two maternity leaves, I've discovered that some companies are willing to let people redesign their positions in a way that will allow them not just to continue their careers, but to accelerate them. It means setting clear goals, forensically analyzing how you spend your time, consciously not doing things that aren't core to meeting your goals, overcommunicating, and then course correcting when required.

Set Clear Goals

In order for any corporate machinery to try to accommodate your career goals, you first need to identify them. If you're not sure what your dreams are, no one can help you realize them. So step back and ask yourself: What do I *really* want?

What are your immediate objectives after you return from your parental leave? What are your long-term goals? Do you want to run your company one day? Or do you want to slow down your career and focus on your family? Or do you hope for some combination of both? All of these options can work—as long as you're honest with yourself and your employer.

If you can't articulate your answers, a parental leave is a great time to reflect on them. Being up with a tiny human at 3 a.m. can give you some time for self-reflection. In my case, it was difficult to envision my long-term goals and to figure out how to achieve them until I took a break from the daily grind on my maternity leaves. During my first leave, I resolved that I wanted to continue in consulting, a field with predominantly male leadership, as a partner at the consulting firm Oliver Wyman. But I also wanted to leave work every day at 6 p.m. to spend time with my family, and I wanted to take August off to travel from my base in London to visit family in Canada.

During my second leave, I decided that I hoped to play a major role in building out our firm's public-sector practice and lead our anti–financial crime business, where I would interact widely and often at the highest levels of our firm, overseeing multiple project teams in multiple countries at any given time. But I also wanted to be able to prioritize my family whenever I needed to. I adjusted my schedule accordingly, so now, instead of leaving work at 6 p.m. every day, I might take off one Monday per month. If I have an emergency doctor's appointment for my child, or if any of a potential million other things crop up unexpectedly with my family life, I can drop work if I need to or I can comfortably agree with my partner that he will handle the situation. In turn, if I have to work in the evening, I don't let it stress me out.

Forensically Analyze How You Spend Your Time

After you've identified your goals, forensically analyze how you spend your time at work and cut out anything that's not aligned with your objectives. Before you go on maternity leave, be clear about what you're working on, whom you're working with, and how you intend to rejoin your team. That way, once you return, you can more easily delegate or drop anything that does not speed up progress.

For people who already work fairly autonomously, this is generally straightforward. But if you are in a more senior position, you'll likely have to say no more often to supporting projects and corporate initiatives that are not directly related to your ambitions. This can be tricky, since there's a risk of being perceived as less committed to your company if you turn down extra work. Still, you must: If you take on too much, you may underdeliver on your work or family commitments, or both. Discuss the right balance with coworkers. People will generally understand if you make it crystal clear how you will still contribute on a broader level, but in a deliberate and agreed-on way by focusing on your goals.

Concentrate on what you *can* do within the time you have and excel at that. When I returned to work following my second maternity leave, I gave up supporting a major part of our business to focus purely on building out our economic crime advisory work with the public sector. Narrowing my focus in this way allowed me to devote the time necessary to develop much more insightful content in my specific area. As a result, we've been able to support the most sophisticated financial centers in improving their financial crime defenses. I miss supporting the other part of our business. But I would make the same decision again.

Overcommunicate

Overcommunicate your aspirations with your employer, colleagues, and family openly and honestly. Share a detailed parental leave plan with your boss that lays out what you want to achieve and the clients and areas that you want to cover. Schedule meetings with your boss before you leave, about a month before you come back, and monthly afterward to discuss how things are going. That way, they can step in to offer support when needed.

It's also important to have continual conversations with your partner at home. Persistently check on how your balance of work and home life is going. In my house, this changes every week. We constantly talk—or frantically text in the middle of the day—about who will pick up our oldest from day care and who can travel on which dates.

Course Correct

Be prepared to adjust. It's impossible to know what it's like to juggle your family and your career until you're in the thick of it. So be open to reassessing your goals and course correct as required.

You may find that you can do more than you expected. When I first came back from maternity leave, I was convinced that I wouldn't be able to commit to multiple client-facing roles. But once I set boundaries and became better at delegating, I found I had more time in my day than anticipated and could gradually take on more.

But accept that things will also not always work out as you'd hoped. I had to take a step back from one global initiative because the team, spread out across multiple time zones, would meet exactly at the time that I wanted to be home with my boys. After sleepless teething nights, I've lost four—yes, four—passports and misplaced countless bank cards and travel coffee cups. At times, our kitchen looks like it was hit by a tornado after we rush out the door in the morning. Don't let these kinds of mishaps cause stress—smile and realize that you're doing the best you can.

Be open and honest when your best-laid plans go awry. That way, the broader team can understand that it is not always an easy journey.

Be a Champion for Others

By bringing your whole self to work, you can encourage your employer to think through, and overcome, the potential obstacles involved in supporting not just your own flexible work arrangements, but also those of others. Actively and visibly support people in a similar position. Support individuals when the risks they have taken have failed and remind the organization, and the individual, that taking risks is a part of being successful—the important thing is to maintain faith in the individual's underlying ability.

Spearhead initiatives with senior leaders in your organization to support new models of working. For example, an initiative called "Men4Change" in our firm is designed to close a gender gap in senior leadership roles. Senior men help to create and assist with customized work arrangements for many high-potential women. A "Boost" program assigns sponsors to support individuals with everything from designing their flexible work arrangements before parental leave to ensuring these agreed-on plans are successfully implemented afterward.

We have not only a moral imperative to make it possible for more people to return to work from parental leave, but also a commercial imperative to develop the best-performing teams. As you navigate your own return, take time to step back and figure out what you really want to accomplish. Find the sponsors who can help you shape and accelerate your career on your own terms. Then pay it forward by being an effective role model and sponsor to other new parents coming up through the ranks after you.

Adapted from content posted on hbr.org, April 9, 2020 (product #H05JR3).

Section 5

All in the Family

Manage Relationships

Bring All of Your Identities to Work

by Carrie Kerpen

Quick Takes

- Set the tone for your team
- Share parts of yourself other than your work self
- Don't be afraid to share failures
- Consider policies or events that build a culture of openness

For years, working parents have discussed and debated bringing our "whole self" to work, or meshing our professional identity with our personal one. Should we try to hide our pregnancies until the third trimester? Should we talk about our children at work? Should we ask for accommodations when we need to go to a parent-teacher conference or soccer game?

A Deloitte study found that 61% of employees "cover" their identities in some way and downplay parts of themselves (such as their identity as a parent) due to fear that they'll be discriminated against or seen as not taking their work seriously enough.[1] And unfortunately, there are studies that support these concerns. One study from Cornell University shows that mothers (but not fathers) are often discriminated against in workplace evaluations.[2] And of course, the perception that mothers are less devoted to their jobs than childless employees is so rampant, it has a name: the "motherhood penalty," or the "maternal wall."

Well, no matter how much we've tried to hide the "other side" of ourselves from our colleagues, Covid-19 has essentially given us no shelter. Aside from essential workers fighting the pandemic on the front lines, many of us are working at home—from weather forecasters and news anchors, to the cast of *SNL*, to the CEOs of the world's largest companies. Did you ever think you'd get to see a corner of Stephen Colbert's home office? I certainly didn't.

This new normal of working from our homes has merged so much more than just our "parent" and "employee" identities, though, because all of us are far more nuanced than that. I'm not just "Work Carrie" and "Home Carrie." I'm a CEO, a mentor, a wife, a mother, and a daughter, too (and most recently, a teacher, chef, and birthday party planner). We've been forced to reveal *all* of our layers, and as scary as that seemed for so long, it's actually been, in my opinion, a major turning point.

Here are some tips for unveiling more of your identities at work, along with some ideas to encourage your team to do the same.

Lead by Example

When my company instituted a "work from home" mandate, I started filming a Facebook Live video every morning in my team's Facebook group as a way to keep them up-to-date and establish some sort of routine. Through these daily videos, my team has *truly* seen every side of me: the frizzy hair, the pajamas, the kids running around in the kitchen, and everything in between. I do talk about work—I recognize accomplishments, give motivational speeches, and keep my team informed on the status of the company. But I don't *just* talk about work. In fact, I talk much less about work than I do about other things, like what I'm baking, how I've been staying active, and how I feel about not being able to visit my mom who is homebound with Multiple Sclerosis.

Why do I do this? Because it's my job as a leader to set the tone for our team. I can't expect my employees to feel comfortable being more open and honest with one another if I'm not doing it myself. And, as it turns out, this is by far their favorite thing I've done (yes, I surveyed them!). From their feedback, it seems that showing them a side—or many sides—of me that they've never seen has allowed them to feel comfortable being open about their own home lives, identities, and challenges.

Share More Than Just the Good Things

In 2013, when my husband, Dave, decided to start his own company and I took over as CEO of Likeable Media, I struggled with impostor syndrome and finding my own identity as a leader. Dave was loud and extroverted, while I was used to handling everything that happened behind the scenes. It took me a while to carve out my niche as a leader and really become comfortable with my own way of doing things.

This wasn't something I revealed to my team at the time, but I do think it was important to share the story with them years later, once I had it figured out (or mostly figured out, because do we ever really have it *all* figured out?). I'm not in the business of pretending everything is always sunshine and rainbows, because the reality is that sometimes things *aren't* great. My team often tells me how much they appreciate my honesty and transparency, because it's alleviated their fears of doing the same.

Of course, it's not always going to be the right time to share something at work—and there may be identities or aspects of your life that you decide never to share. But there is power in vulnerability; often it's when you share those types of struggles with others that a new level of understanding and trust develops.

Actively Encourage

Some individuals or teams may need more direct encouragement than just modeling the behavior you'd like them to adopt.

Last year, I made "balance" one of my company's core values. When I announced this to my team, I stressed the fact that I *want* them to have lives outside of work. And I want them to feel comfortable sharing those lives with one another. I stated my belief that work should be a *part* of your life, not your whole life. What's most important, though, is that this emphasis on balance is not just on the surface. Our policies back it up, too—things like unlimited paid time off, summer Fridays, generous parental leave policies, and a monthly "Balance Bucks" stipend to spend on classes, activities, or things that improve their home office setups.

You don't need to alter the values that have been at the core of your company since day one, but you may need to make a more active effort to prove that openness is important to you. This could mean something grand such as hosting events like a quarterly team retreat where employees are encouraged to share something about their lives or interests outside of work. Or it could be something simple, like devoting 10 minutes of a weekly meeting to having a team member talk about a cause that's important to them.

Creating a culture where everyone feels free to be themselves will help ease tensions and increase understanding. Maybe you were frustrated by a colleague who was leaving work early once a week, but then you learned their child was struggling emotionally and had to attend weekly therapy sessions. Maybe another colleague seemed unapproachable or short-tempered until you discovered they were dealing with a death in their family. Maybe you learned about what makes someone tick or what inspires them, which helped you get them to open up during a brainstorming session.

When your team feels comfortable bringing all their identities to work, you'll see a boost in synergy, trust, and productivity. But most important, your team will develop empathy and deeper ties. And when you're not worried about covering an aspect of who you are, it frees up more headspace to focus on work that matters to you—and your organization.

Adapted from "Parents, Bring Your Whole Self to Work," on hbr.org, July 9, 2020 (product #H05Q53).

How Dual-Career Couples Make It Work

by Jennifer Petriglieri

Quick Takes

- Communicate about values, boundaries, and fears
- Negotiate roles and divide family commitments
- Support each other through periods of reflection and exploration
- Identify the opportunity in loss
- Address regrets and developmental asymmetries

C amille and Pierre met in their early forties after each one's marriage had ended. Both were deeply committed to their careers and to their new relationship. Camille, an accountant, had felt pressured by her ex-husband to slow her progress toward partnership at her firm. Pierre, a production manager at an automotive company, was embroiled in a bitter divorce from his wife, who had given up her career to accommodate the geographic moves that his required. (As with the other couples I've profiled in this article, these aren't their real names.) Bruised by their past experiences, they agreed to place their careers on an equal footing. Initially things went smoothly, but two years in, Camille began to feel trapped on a professional path that she realized she had chosen because "that was what the smart kids did."

Mindful of their pact, Pierre calmly listened to her doubts and encouraged her to explore alternatives. But as the months wore on, he began to feel weighed down as he juggled providing emotional support to Camille, navigating their complex family logistics (both had children from their former marriages), and succeeding in his demanding job. When he began to question his own career direction, he wondered how the two of them could manage to change course. They couldn't afford to take time out from work, nor could they take much time to reflect and keep their family and relationship afloat. Frustrated and exhausted, both wondered how they could continue to find meaning and fulfillment in their lives.

Dual-earner couples are on the rise. According to Pew Research, in 63% of couples with children in the United States, for example, both partners work (this figure is slightly higher in the EU).[1] Many of these are *dual-career couples*: Both partners are highly educated, work full-time in demanding professional or managerial jobs, and see themselves on an upward path in their roles. For these couples, as for Pierre and Camille, work is a primary source of identity and a primary channel for ambition. Evidence is mounting from sociological research that when both partners dedicate themselves to work and to home life, they reap benefits such as increased economic freedom, a more satisfying relationship, and a lower-than-average chance of divorce.

Because their working lives and personal lives are deeply intertwined, however, dual-career couples face unique challenges. How do they decide whose job to relocate for, when it's OK for one partner to make a risky career change, or who will leave work early to pick up a sick child from school? How can they give family commitments—and each other—their full attention while both of them are working in demanding roles? And when one of them wants to undertake a professional reinvention, what does that mean for the other? They must work out these questions together, in a way that lets both thrive in love and work. If they don't, regrets and imbalances quickly build up, threatening to hinder their careers, dissolve their relationship, or both.

Many of these challenges are well recognized, and I've previously written in HBR about how companies can adapt their talent strategies to account for some of them ("Talent Management and the Dual-Career Couple," May–June, 2018). But for the couples themselves, little guidance is available. Most advice treats major career decisions as if one is flying solo, without a partner, children, or aging parents to consider. When it's for couples, it focuses on their relationship, not how that intersects with their professional dreams, or it addresses how to balance particular trade-offs, such as careers versus family, or how to prioritize partners' work travel. What couples need is a more comprehensive approach for managing the moments when commitments and aspirations clash.

My personal experience in a dual-career couple, and my realization that little systematic academic research had been done in this area, prompted a six-year investigation into the lives of more than 100 dual-career couples, resulting in my book, *Couples That Work.*[2] The people I studied come from around the world, range in age from mid-twenties to mid-sixties, and represent a range of professions, from corporate executive to entrepreneur to worker in the nonprofit sector. My research revealed that dual-career couples overcome their challenges by directly addressing deeper psychological and social forces—such as struggles for power and control; personal hopes, fears, and losses; and assumptions and cultural expectations about the roles partners should play in each other's lives and what it means to have a good relationship or career.

I also discovered that three transition points typically occur during dual-career couples' working and love lives, when those forces are particularly strong. It is during these transitions, I found, that some couples craft a way to thrive in love and work, while others are plagued by conflict and regret. By understanding each transition and knowing what questions to ask each other and what traps to avoid, dual-career couples can emerge stronger, fulfilled in their relationships and in their careers. "A Guide to Couple Contracting" can help partners identify, address, and find common ground.

Transition 1: Working as a Couple

When Jamal and Emily met, in their late twenties, trade-offs were the last thing on their minds. They were full of energy, optimistic, and determined to live life to the fullest. Jamal, a project manager in a civil engineering firm, traveled extensively for work and was given increasingly complex projects to lead, while Emily, who worked at a clothing company, had just been promoted to her first management role. They saw each other mostly on weekends, which they often spent on wilderness hiking adventures. They married 18 months after their first date.

Then, in the space of three months, their world changed dramatically. While Emily was pregnant with their first child, Jamal's boss asked him to run a critical infrastructure project in Mexico. Jamal agreed to spend three weeks out of every month in Mexico City; designating some of his pay raise to extra childcare would allow Emily to keep working in Houston, where they lived. But when their daughter, Aisha, was born two weeks early, Jamal was stuck in the Mexico City airport waiting for a flight home. Soon Emily, who was single-handedly managing Aisha, her job, and their home, discovered that the additional childcare wasn't enough; she felt overburdened and unappreciated. Jamal was exhausted by the relentless travel and the stress of the giant new project; he felt isolated, incompetent, and guilty.

After many arguments, they settled on what they hoped was a practical solution: Because Jamal earned more, Emily took a smaller project role that she could manage remotely, and she and Aisha joined him in Mexico. But Emily felt disconnected from her company's head office and was passed over for a promotion, and eventually she grew resentful of the arrangement. By the time Jamal's boss began talking about his next assignment, their fighting had become intense.

A Guide to Couple Contracting

Drawing on my research, I've developed a systematic tool to help dual-career couples who are facing any of the three transitions described in this chapter. I call it *couple contracting*, because to shape their joint path, partners must address three areas—values, boundaries, and fears—and find common ground in each. Values define the direction of your path, boundaries set its borders, and fears reveal the potential cliffs to avoid on either side. Sharing a clear view in these three domains will make it easier to negotiate and overcome the challenges you encounter together.

First, take some time on your own to write down your thoughts about each of the three areas. Then share your reflections with each other. Listen to and acknowledge each other's responses, resisting any temptation to diminish or discount your partner's fears. Next, note where you have common ground and where your values and boundaries diverge. No couple has perfect overlap in those two areas, but if they are too divergent, negotiate a middle ground. If, for example, one of you could tolerate living apart for a period but the other could not, you'll need to shape a boundary that works for both of you.

A Guide to Couple Contracting

Values

When our choices and actions align with our values, we feel content; when they don't, we feel stressed and unhappy. Openly discussing your values will make it easier to make choices that align with them. For example, if you and your partner know you both greatly value family time, you'll be clear that neither of you should take a job requiring 70-hour workweeks.

Questions to ask each other:

What makes you happy and proud? What gives you satisfaction? What makes for a good life?

Boundaries

Setting clear boundaries together allows you to make big decisions more easily. Consider three types of boundaries: place, time, and presence.

Questions to ask each other:

Are there places where you'd love to work and live at some point in your life? Are there places you'd prefer to avoid? Understanding that we may sometimes have to put in more hours than we'd like, how much work is too much? How would you feel about our taking jobs in different cities and living apart for a period? For how long? How much work travel is too much, and how will we juggle travel between us?

Fears

Monitoring each other's fears can help you spot trouble and take preventive action before your relationship enters dangerous territory. Many fears are endemic to relationships and careers: You may worry that your partner's family will encroach on your relationship, that over time the two of you will grow apart, that your partner will have an affair, that you will have to sacrifice your career for your partner's, or that you may not be able to have children. But sharing these fears allows you to build greater empathy and support. If you know that your partner is worried about the role of your parents in your lives, for example, you are more likely to manage the boundary between them and your partnership sensitively. Likewise, if you are interested in a risky career transition but worried that financial commitments would prevent it, you might agree to cut back on family spending in order to build a buffer.

Questions to ask each other:

What are your concerns for the future? What's your biggest fear about how our relationship and careers interact? What do you dread might happen in our lives?

The first transition that dual-career couples must navigate often comes as a response to the first major life event they face together—typically a big career opportunity, the arrival of a child, or the merger of families from previous relationships. To adapt, the partners must negotiate how to prioritize their careers and divide family commitments. Doing so in a way that lets them both thrive requires an underlying shift: They must move from having parallel, independent careers and lives to having interdependent ones.

My research shows two common traps for couples negotiating their way through their first transition.

Concentrating exclusively on the practical

In the first transition in particular, couples often look for logistical solutions to their challenges, as Jamal and Emily did when they arranged for extra childcare and negotiated how many weekends Jamal would be home. This focus is understandable—such problems are tangible, and the underlying psychological and social tensions are murky and anxiety provoking—but it prolongs the struggle, because those tensions remain unresolved.

Instead of simply negotiating over calendars and to-do lists, couples must understand, share, and discuss the emotions, values, and fears underlying their decisions. Talking about feelings as well as practicalities can help them mitigate and manage them.

Basing decisions primarily on money

Many couples focus on economic gain as they decide where to live, whose career to prioritize, and who will do the majority of the childcare. But as sensible (and sometimes unavoidable) as this is, it often means that their decisions end up at odds with their other values and desires.

Few people live for financial gain alone. In their careers they are also motivated by continual learning and being given greater responsibilities. Outside work, they want to spend time with their children and pursue personal interests. Couples may be attracted to a location because of proximity to extended family, the quality of life it affords, or their ability to build a strong community. Basing the decision to move to Mexico on Jamal's higher salary meant that he and Emily ignored their other interests, feeding their discontent.

Couples who are successful discuss the foundations and the structure of their joint path forward. First, they must come to some agreement on core aspects of their relationship: their values, boundaries, and fears. Negotiating and finding common ground in these areas helps them navigate difficult decisions because they can agree on criteria in advance. Doing this together is important; couples that make this arrangement work, I found, make choices openly and jointly, rather than implicitly and for each other. The ones I studied who had never addressed their core criteria struggled in later transitions, because those criteria never go away.

Next, couples must discuss how to prioritize their careers and divide family commitments. Striving for 50/50 is not always the best option; neither must one decide to always give the other's career priority.

There are three basic models to consider: (1) In *primary-secondary*, one partner's career takes priority over the other's for the duration of their working lives. The primary person dedicates more time to work and less to the family, and their professional commitments (and geographic requirements) usually come before the secondary person's. (2) In *turn taking*, the partners agree to periodically swap the primary and secondary positions. (3) In *double-primary*, they continually juggle two primary careers.

My research shows that couples can feel fulfilled in their careers and relationships whichever model they pursue, as long as it aligns with their values and they openly discuss and explicitly agree on their options. Couples who pursue the third option are often the most successful, although it's arguably the most difficult, precisely because they are forced to address conflicts most frequently.

To work past their deadlock, Emily and Jamal finally discussed what really mattered to them beyond financial success. They identified pursuit of their chosen careers, proximity to nature, and a stable home for Aisha where they could both actively parent her. They admitted their fears of growing apart, and in response agreed to an important restriction: They would live in the same city and would limit work travel to 25% of their time. They agreed to place their geographic boundaries around North America, and Jamal suggested that they both draw circles on a map around the cities where they felt they could make a home and have two careers. Their conversations and mapping exercise eventually brought them to a resolution—and a new start in Atlanta, where they would pursue a double-primary model. Three years later they are progressing in their careers, happy in their family life, and expecting a second child.

Transition 2: Reinventing Themselves

Psychological theory holds that early in life many people follow career and personal paths that conform to the expectations of their parents, friends, peers, and society, whereas in their middle years many feel a pressing need for *individuation,* or breaking free of those expectations to become authors of their own lives. This tends to happen in people's forties, regardless of their relationship status, and is part of a process colloquially known as the midlife crisis.

We tend to think of a midlife crisis mostly in personal terms (a husband leaves his wife, for example, and buys a sports car), but in dual-career couples, the intense focus on professional success means that the partners' job tracks come under scrutiny as well. This combined personal and professional crisis forms the basis of the second transition. Camille and Pierre, whose story began this article, were in the midst of it.

As each partner wrestles with self-redefinition, the two often bump up against long-settled arrangements they have made and the identities, relationship, and careers they have crafted together. Some of those arrangements—whose career takes precedence, for example—may need to be reconsidered to allow one partner to quit a job and explore alternatives. It may be painful to question the choices they made together during the previous transition and have since built their lives around. This can be threatening to a relationship; it's not uncommon for one partner to interpret the other's desire to rethink past career choices as an inclination to rethink the relationship as well, or even to potentially end it. Couples who handle this transition well find ways to connect with and support each other through what can feel like a very solitary process.

The second transition often begins—as it did for Camille and Pierre—when one partner reexamines a career or life path. That person must reflect on questions such as: What led me to this impasse? Why did I make the choices I made? Who am I? What do I desire from life? Whom do I want to become? They should also take time to explore alternative paths, through networking events, job shadowing, secondments, volunteer work, and so forth. Such individual reflection and exploration can lead couples to the first trap of the second transition.

Mistrust and defensiveness

Living with a partner who is absorbed in exploring new paths can feel threatening. Painful questions surface: Why is my partner not satisfied? Is this a career problem or a relationship problem? Am I to blame? Why do they need new people? Am I no longer enough? These doubts can lead to mistrust and defensiveness, which may push the exploring partner to withdraw further from the relationship, making the other even more mistrustful and defensive, until eventually the relationship itself becomes an obstacle to individuation, rather than a space for it.

In such a situation, people should first be open about their concerns and let their partners reassure them that the angst is not about them or the relationship. Next, they should adopt what literary critics call *suspension of disbelief*—that is, faith that the things they have doubts about will unfold in interesting ways and are worth paying attention to. This attitude will both enrich their own lives and make their partners' exploration easier.

Finally, they should understand their role as supporters. Psychologists call this role in a relationship the *secure base* and see it as vital to the other partner's growth.

Originally identified and described by the psychologist John Bowlby, the secure base allows us to stretch ourselves by stepping outside our comfort zone while someone by our side soothes our anxieties about doing so. Without overly interfering, supporters should encourage their partners' exploration and reflection, even if it means moving away from the comfortable relationship they've already established.

Being a secure base for a partner presents its own trap, however.

Asymmetric support

In some couples one partner consistently supports the other without receiving support in return. That's what happened to Camille and Pierre. Pierre's experience in his former marriage, in which his wife gave up her career for his, made him determined to support Camille, and he initially stepped up to be a secure base for her. Their lives were so packed, however, that Camille had trouble finding the energy to return the favor. The result was that her exploration and reflection became an impediment to Pierre's, creating a developmental and relationship deadlock. It is important to remember that acting as a secure base does not mean annihilating your own wishes, atoning for past selfishness, or being perfect. You can be a wonderful supporter for your partner while requesting support in return and taking time for yourself. In fact, that will most likely make you a far better (and less resentful) supporter.

In my research I found that couples who make it through their second transition are those in which the partners encourage each other to do this work—even if it means that one of them is exploring and providing support at the same time.

Once the exploring partner has had a chance to determine what they want in a career, a life, or a relationship, the next step is to make it happen—as a couple. Couples need to renegotiate the roles they play in each other's lives. Take Matthew and James, another pair I spoke with, who had risen through the professional ranks in their 18 years together. When Matthew realized that he wanted to get off what he called the success train—on which he felt like a mere passenger—both he and James had to let go of their identity as a power couple and revisit the career-prioritization agreement they had forged during their first transition. Initially Matthew was reluctant to talk to James about his doubts, because he questioned whether James would still love him if he changed direction. When they started discussing this, however, they realized that their identity as a power couple had trapped them in a dynamic in which both needed to succeed but neither could outshine the other. Acknowledging and renegotiating this unspoken arrangement allowed James to shoot for his first senior executive position and Matthew to transition into the nonprofit sector. The time and care they took to answer their existential questions and renegotiate the roles they played in each other's lives set them up for a renewed period of growth in their careers and in their relationship.

Transition 3: Loss and Opportunity

Attending her mother's funeral was one of the most difficult experiences of Norah's life. It was the culmination of two years of immense change for her and her husband, Jeremy, who were in their late fifties. The change began when their fathers unexpectedly passed away within five weeks of each other, and they became caregivers for Norah's ailing mother just as their children were leaving the nest and their own careers were in flux.

' Jeremy is a digital visual artist. His studio's main projects were ending because a big client was moving on. Though he was sad, he had become confident enough to feel excited about whatever might come next. Norah had been working for the same small agricultural machinery business for 26 years; she had once wanted to change careers but felt that she couldn't do so while Jeremy was relying on her for emotional and logistical support. Now she was being asked to take an early retirement deal. She felt thrown on the scrap heap despite her long commitment to the company. No career, no parents, no children to care for—who was she now? She felt disoriented and adrift.

The third transition is typically triggered by shifting roles later in life, which often create a profound sense of loss. Careers plateau or decline; bodies are no longer what they once were; children, if there are any, leave home. Sometimes one partner's career is going strong while the other's begins to ebb. Having raced through decades of career growth and child-rearing, couples wake up with someone who may have changed since the time they fell in love. They may both feel that way. These changes again raise fundamental questions of identity: Who am I now? Who do I want to be for the rest of my life?

Although loss usually triggers it, the third transition heralds opportunity. Chances for late-in-life reinvention abound, especially in today's world. Life expectancy is rising across the globe, and older couples may have several decades of reasonably good health and freedom from intensive parenting responsibilities. As careers and work become more flexible, especially for those with experience, people can engage in multiple activities more easily than previous generations could—combining advisory or consulting work with board service, for example. Their activities often include giving back to the community, leaving some kind of legacy, mentoring younger generations, rediscovering passions of their youth, or dedicating themselves more to friendships.

Their task in the third transition is to again reinvent themselves—this time in a way that is both grounded in past accomplishments and optimistic about possibilities for the future. They must mourn the old, welcome the new, figure out how the two fit together, and adjust their life path to support who they want to become.

One thing that struck me when I spoke to couples in their third transition is that it's most powerful when partners reinvent themselves together—not just reflecting jointly, as in the other transitions, but actually taking on a new activity or project side by side. When one is curious about a partner's life and work as well as one's own, an immense capacity for mutual revitalization is unlocked. I met many couples who were charting new paths out of this transition that involved a merging of their work—launching a new business together, for example.

The third transition also has its traps.

Unfinished business

For better or for worse, earlier relational patterns, approaches, decisions, and assumptions will influence how a couple's third transition unfolds. I found that the most common challenge in managing this transition was overcoming regret about perceived failures in the way the partners had "worked" as a couple—how they had prioritized their careers, or how each partner had supported the other's development (or not).

To move through the third transition, couples must acknowledge how they got where they are and commit to playing new roles for each other in the future. For example, Norah and Jeremy had become stuck in a pattern in which Norah was Jeremy's supporter. By recognizing this—and both their roles in cementing it—they were able to become more mutually supportive.

Narrow horizons

By the time a couple reaches the third transition, they will probably have suffered their fair share of disappointments and setbacks. They may be tired from years of taking care of others, or just from staying on the treadmill. As their roles shift and doubts about their identities grow, reinvention may be beyond consideration. In addition, because previous generations retired earlier, didn't live as long, and didn't have access to the gig economy, many couples lack role models for what reinvention can look like at this stage of life. If they don't deliberately broaden their horizons, they miss opportunities to discover themselves anew.

So couples must explore again. Even more than in the second transition, they need to flirt with multiple possibilities. Like healthy children, who are curious about the world, themselves, and those around them, they can actively seek new experiences and experiment, avoid taking things for granted, and constantly ask "Why?" Most of us suppress our childhood curiosity as life progresses and responsibilities pile up. But it is vital to overcome the fear of leaving behind a cherished self and allow ambitions and priorities to diversify. Exploring at this stage is rejuvenating.

Shifts in people's roles and identities offer a perfect excuse to question their current work, life, and loves. Many people associate exploring with looking for new options, which is surely important. But it's also about questioning assumptions and approaches and asking, "Is this really how things need to be?"

Having rebalanced their support for each other, Norah and Jeremy could open up to new possibilities. Having earned financial security from their previous work, they sought reinvention not only in their careers but also in their wider roles in the world. Encouraging each other, they both transitioned to portfolio working lives. Jeremy became a freelance digital visual artist, took a part-time role teaching young art students at a local college, and dedicated more time to his passion of dinghy sailing. Norah retrained to be a counselor working with distressed families and began volunteering at a local agricultural museum. With these new opportunities and more time for each other and their friends, they felt newfound satisfaction with their work and with their relationship.

Conclusion

The challenges couples face at each transition are different but linked. In their first transition, the partners accommodate to a major life event by negotiating the roles they will play in each other's lives. Over time those roles become constraining and spark the restlessness and questioning that lead to the second transition. To successfully navigate the third transition, couples must address regrets and developmental asymmetries left over from their first two transitions.

No one right path or solution exists for meeting these challenges. Although the 50/50 marriage—in which housework and childcare are divided equally between the partners, and their careers are perfectly synced— may seem like a noble ideal, my research suggests that instead of obsessively trying to maintain an even "score," dual-career couples are better off being relentlessly curious, communicative, and proactive in making choices about combining their lives.

Reprinted from Harvard Business Review, *originally published September 2019 (product #R1905B).*

14

Being a Two-Career Couple Requires a Long-Term Plan

by Avivah Wittenberg-Cox

Quick Takes

- Consider career choices from a long-term perspective
- Identify your current relationship model
- Acknowledge the advantages and risks of the path you choose

"We learned to take the long view, mostly because we didn't have any other choice," says Kate, now in her sixties and busy investing in the next generation of entrepreneurs. "Both sticking to our full-time corporate jobs or one of us becoming a full-time parent weren't attractive options to us. We wanted to change the model, not just flip it."

Kate and her husband, Matthew, were a classic dual-career couple. They met in business school, married, and settled into two demanding corporate jobs. But Kate quickly saw that there were too many layers in her firm to get to the top anytime soon. Matthew had a quicker route in his flatter organization. When the couple decided to have children, they sat down and strategized together. How could they design two careers that could give them both what they wanted: meaningful work, financial security, and a great family?

One of their innovations was to plan a lifetime family career—together. Most of us are well meaning in wanting to support our partner and their careers. But thinking about two careers individually and then trying to marry them together is often a design challenge. Matthew and Kate started with designing a life and retrofitted it to identify careers that might deliver it. They devised a single vision for themselves as a couple—and the family they had just started. They thought of it as a team vision, as they might at work. What were their respective strengths, and their respective dreams? How could they use each other to guarantee the success of their broader vision, while minimizing some of the risks they might bump into along their road? It wasn't so much the plan that helped them, they found. It was the conversation and the search for complementarity. They were each agreeing to contribute to building something to fit them both, over a life span.

In their thirties, they decided that Kate would leave her corporate job to gain the flexibility she prioritized short-term to care for their two young children. Matthew would continue in his corporate role to cover this life phase's financial needs. She would launch a business she had identified as having serious potential and test run it. If it worked, he could join her later down the road to scale and sell it and be able to reinvent themselves again.

And it worked.

From the Sum of Two to the Power of Two

Dual-income couples are the norm: Over two-thirds of couples in Canada and the U.K., and 60% of couples in the U.S.[1] Your partner may be your most significant career asset.

Not only can your working spouse mitigate risks like being made redundant, they can also serve as a trampoline to allow you a shot at your dream, whether it's a novel or a nonprofit, a startup or a soap opera, and whether you grab it in your thirties or your sixties.

It wasn't possible in an earlier era of single-earner families, where the financial burden historically (and often still psychically) fell to the man. Nor is it true today among the growing number of couples who simply flip the gender roles but still stick to the same model (nor among single-parent households, dominated by women). These options have little flexibility and less security in increasingly volatile economic times.

But for too many dual-career couples, even in an era of supposed equality, two individuals can end up competing for short-term trade-offs rather than cooperating for longer-term, mutually beneficial gains. Couples end up negotiating, based on current realities, rather than pacing themselves for the long (and lengthening) haul. This translates into decisions based on who has the higher income, the assignment abroad, or the babies. How many couples decide that one parent will stay home because the cost of childcare is more than one parent's (still usually mom's) income? They forget to calculate the impact of that choice on that parent's career, on their lifetime earning potential (opting out can cost up to $1 million in lost income), and on the couple's opportunities to switch roles or combine them.

As careers morph into 50-year marathons rather than 30-year sprints, we may also want to think of couple careers over much longer time frames. We still let too many decisions made in our thirties seal our professional fate for decades. How much more reassuring to know that you can hand the baton back and forth—and still finish the race in style.

Flex Your Mind to Find Your Model

For many, there is more focus on innovation at work than at home. So invite a little brainstorming into your family boardroom (the dinner table). What's your model? Are you both happy with your respective roles as currently defined? Is there a dream one or both of you feel it's time to dust off and discuss?

Here are some of the models I've seen couples define, negotiate, and enjoy, sometimes only for a phase, sometimes for a lifetime. All of them work, as long as both halves are aligned and agreed—at least for the moment.

- **Single career**—a historic classic. One partner has the career that defines everything else. The spouse and children follow that career. This often allows for high salaries and gives one partner total work focus. The other partner is open to all other roles, without having to worry about income. But the couple is more at risk of unexpected and complete loss of income. The nonworking partner will find it much harder to recover from eventual separations or divorce, and may not be putting anything aside for retirement. One of the challenges for many senior women (most of whom have working partners) is that they sit on senior teams dominated by men with nonworking wives. This puts them at a competitive disadvantage when the team cultures created by single-career spouses lean to the 24/7. Because they can.

- **Lead career**—a version of single career. One career is clearly dominant and will define where the couple lives, where they move to, and so on. The other partner has a more flexible career role, even part-time or freelance. This model has the same advantages and some mitigation of the disadvantages of the single-career model. For example, Jo followed her oil executive partner around the globe and turned her trailing spouse role into a profession. She wrote books about how to reinvent yourself and became an online editor and writer's coach.

- **Alternators**—many couples opt for what they see as an egalitarian alternation of opportunity. Each has first dibs for the next promotion or geographic move, and the other agrees to adjust in function. This doesn't always mean the other partner follows, with family in tow. Sometimes families stay in one place, and the roving partner commutes a lot. In multinational companies, many spouses live apart, sometimes for years. This approach can get a bit transactional if it's held to too inflexibly. When "my turn" becomes absolute, couples lose the balance they were aiming to build. Helen and her husband, Rob, a highly successful and very visible pair of CEOs, alternated weeks throughout the year. Each would be able to fully focus on work, travel, and urgencies one week out of two. The other week, they'd have primary responsibility for everything else. It allowed them to be able to enjoy both roles fully and regularly.

- Parallelograms—two parallel, high-powered careers, commonly known as "power couples." Often mutually reinforcing, these careers have professional networks and knowledge that feed each other. These couples love to talk shop and share what's going on in their mutual careers, because it nourishes the other. Parallelograms can learn from each other and buy from each other's companies. Juliet and Andrew run two separate but related businesses, where one heads the for-profit arm and the other the nonprofit arm. Together, they make a successful combination. The risk here is usually for the family, which may not get as much attention as they'd like. Their parents are too excited talking to each other. Two big careers are particularly frustrating to employers these days, as these couples are increasingly less mobile geographically. The seniority of the other partner's job is not always easy to replicate or transfer.

- Complements—diversity in couple careers can be as beneficial as diversity in any team. Couples with very different kinds of careers, with different phases, peak periods, and time frames, often find life a bit easier to sort out. Pressure points are often not at the same time of the year or at the same phase of life, so they can be more easily managed. Complements cover a vast range of occupations, from the corporate career and the academic, to the entrepreneur and the writer. George and Anne used time shifts as their differentiator, with one being a night nurse, the other an engineer by day. Their time home overlapped for breakfast and dinner. Juliet was a flexible freelancer when her children were young, and her husband, John, loved his corporate work in social responsibility. When their children were older, her business took off. John retired early from his successful career and was able to travel the globe with his wife and her growing business. Another advantage of very different tracks is that it relieves some of the competition that can exist between careers that are similar. Two lawyers or two consultants who progress at very different speeds, especially if there are childcare choices involved, can lead to conflict. Complements tend to have different success criteria and life cycles, which can work together well.

Whatever model you choose, the secret lies in the codesign. You may move from one model to another over the course of ever-longer careers, and that may even be part of the plan. But it helps to be able to put a name on what you're both doing and acknowledge the advantages and risks of each option at different phases of life. Dual careers offer flexibility, security, and options. Each spouse has a supportive partner who shares a life vision and is as invested in your career choices as they are in their own. That is exponentially beneficial to both.

Adapted from content posted on hbr.org, February 26, 2018 (product #H046QX).

15

A Guide to Balancing Eldercare and Career

by Liz O'Donnell

Quick Takes

- Acknowledge the many roles you play
- Identify the support you'll need
- Explore what benefits your company offers
- Share the basic facts with your boss
- Consider your legacy as a child

W hen my parents were both in their 80s and requiring more and more support from me, I found balancing their needs with my career incredibly challenging. For starters, I thought I was the only one at work who was struggling with eldercare. When my coworkers went out on parental leave to have babies, we would throw office showers and share our best parenting tips. When they returned, we would coo over the baby pictures they proudly displayed on their desks and offer assistance in juggling childcare and career. But when my parents stopped driving and got sick, and I started taking time off to care for them, no one at the office had a party for me. No one offered advice. No one even knew.

Despite the lack of support, it turns out I wasn't alone. There are an estimated 50 million people who have worked and provided care to an aging family member.[1] These family caregivers, especially the women, often find they need to switch to less demanding jobs, take time off, or quit work in order to make time for their caregiving duties. With 10,000 people turning 65 every day, and a predicted shortage of paid caregivers in the next few years, the number of working daughters and sons is only expected to increase. And while the average caregiver to an aging parent is a woman in her late 40s, more and more Millennials are assuming eldercare responsibilities.

Fortunately, there are steps you can take to better balance the competing demands of caring for your parents, working, and raising kids.

Accept your role as caregiver

One of the many things that makes managing eldercare more difficult than childcare is the fact that most of us don't plan for the role. We often plan in advance to have children, thinking through the best time to start a family, how it might impact our career, and what resources we'll need for support. Even those who don't plan still generally have nine months to prepare. That's not the case with eldercare. Often it starts with helping your parents with a few small tasks like grocery shopping or paying bills, and before you know it, you've taken on driving your parents to their doctor appointments and assisting with medication management and dressing and bathing. Or, your parents have a medical emergency, and overnight you become their caregiver. No matter how it starts, take a moment to acknowledge the fact that you have taken on a new and significant role.

Brainstorm what kind of support you think you could use

Once you acknowledge and accept that you have a new role, you can start to identify what supports you need to put in place and what accommodations, if any, you need to make at work. Like the working parent who outlines a plan for incorporating a child into their life, think about what you need to make your career and care responsibilities more compatible. Do you require a few extra hours in the morning to get your parent set up for the day or to wait for a paid caregiver to arrive for a shift? Do you need to leave early to accompany your parent to doctor appointments? Do you need the flexibility to work remotely so that you can be at their bedside at a hospital or hospice home? You're more likely to succeed if you're clear about what you need to make work and life fit.

Likewise, think about what *won't* be helpful. This will help you prepare to turn down suggestions that won't work for you. For example, your boss may suggest that you stop traveling or give up a high-profile assignment. But you might find work to be a respite from caregiving or a welcome challenge to take your mind off your parent's health issues, so while well intended, such an offer may have an adverse effect on your well-being. Also, know that as your parent's needs change as they age or an illness progresses, or perhaps if they transition from home to a senior living facility, that your support needs will change too.

Do your homework

Understand what options are available to you as you seek to integrate your caregiving role into your professional role. Start with your company handbook or human resources intranet. Does your company offer any caregiving benefits such as access to a geriatric care manager, or backup eldercare for when your parent cannot be left alone? What policies exist for flexible work arrangements like working from home, staggered start times, or job sharing? Does your company have a paid-time-off policy? Is the company eligible for the Family Medical Leave Act, which allows employees to take up to 12 workweeks of leave in one year to care for a family member with a serious health condition? Are you eligible?

Once you've done some research, look beyond the policies to assess your company culture. Note what benefits, if any, the management team does or doesn't use. Notice what flexible options your peers are taking advantage of. It's helpful to understand the unwritten rules of your company as well as the official policies as you navigate how best to access the flexibility you may need.

Decide how much to disclose

Once you've researched your company's policies and approach to caregiving and flexibility, determine how much of your personal situation you want to share. Ideally, you'll feel comfortable talking to your manager or human resources department about your caregiving situation. If they're aware, they can help you access support. You never want to surprise your boss. By disclosing some details of your situation, you give your company time to prepare for when you may have to take time off or leave work with no notice. That said, it's not always prudent to share information about your personal life at work. That's where your observations on company culture come in. Think about how secure you feel in your job and your company's tolerance for work-life issues. In some cases, sharing the fact that you have challenges outside the office may cause managers to view you as a weak link or to withhold assignments and promotions.

If you do decide to disclose that you have eldercare responsibilities, or you want to access particular benefits, stick to the basic facts. You don't have to share details about a diagnosis or overshare your personal concerns about paying your parents' medical bills or dealing with dysfunctional sibling dynamics. Make some recommendations on how best to cover your work in the event you cannot do it and be prepared to ask for any support you think you may need.

Build trust every day

Trust is your most important currency at work. It's what you trade for the flexibility you need. To earn and keep that trust, consider how you're showing up at work and actively manage your reputation. For example, if you know that you'll have to take personal calls from work, tell your colleagues up front that you may need to step out of the office for a few minutes or that you'll be checking your phone during a meeting. If you're working remotely, make sure you have what you need to be productive, like a reliable Wi-Fi connection and access to your files. Continue to respond in a timely manner to emails, Slack messages, and voice mail. Finally, make it easy for coworkers to fill in for you if needed. Keep your assignments organized. Copy team members on important correspondence and file documents where others can access them, such as on the company server or Google Drive.

If you do have to leave early or take unplanned time off, make it easy for colleagues to cover for you. Share status updates on your assignments including where to find important information and how to reach project stakeholders. It's less important to share the details of your caregiving emergency and more important to share details on what needs to be done, how to do it, and when you think you'll be available to check in and answer any questions that may arise.

Marshal support

Look for ways to build a support network. As a society, we have come a long way in a short time in supporting working parents. We need to do the same for workers with aging parents. Consider starting a support group at work for adult children. Talk to your human resource department and ask if the company will sponsor a special interest group to help caregivers manage their career and care challenges. If the company isn't willing, ask other caregivers to meet for lunch to brainstorm ideas on managing care needs and trade resources. The sooner we make eldercare visible at work, the sooner we will start to create better solutions for making the two compatible.

Focus on the long game

Most important, keep in mind that your role as a working child is only one phase of your career. Spend some time thinking about what you want your life to look like post-caregiving. What are your long-term goals for your career, financial security, family, and personal legacy as a daughter or son? As a working caregiver, you are constantly choosing between career and care: travel for work or stay home; pursue a promotion or work part-time, go to the hospital or attend the meeting? Let your long-term goals guide you as you make those decisions. When you're clear about what's most important to you, you can make smart decisions about how to navigate this challenging time in your career and life.

Adapted from "Balancing Work and Eldercare Through the Coronavirus Crisis," March 31, 2020 (H05ICW).

Section 6

Don't Go
It Alone

Get Support

16

Working Parents Need a "Parenting Posse"

by Alison Beard

Quick Takes

- Take time to engage with a wide variety of parents
- Offer to help drive a kid to practice or contribute to a class party
- Be generous with your encouragement and what's worked for you
- Ask for help—even at the last minute
- Listen and learn from other parents

On a typical Monday, at the start of a super-busy workweek for me, one of my mom friends, Heather, picked up my daughter from school and kept her into the evening. On Tuesday, another mom friend, Nicolle, drove my son to his 5:45 p.m. basketball practice. On Wednesday, Tricia handled the cooking-class-to-home carpool. On Thursday, Sarah chaperoned both of our daughters at skating. And, on Friday, Rebecca helped me think through a tricky situation at the office.

I'm so grateful to have what every parent with a job outside the home needs: a parenting posse. This is a group of fellow moms and dads—at my kids' school, in our neighborhood, and at the office—who support me in the extremely messy business of balancing my work and home lives well.

You might not think that an upper-middle-class knowledge worker like me would need this help. My husband and I both have busy jobs but relatively flexible schedules. We're able to work from home. Right now, our business travel is limited. And we can afford to pay an afternoon sitter to assist with childcare and driving. But I suspect that we would struggle mightily to maintain our careers if we couldn't call on others to fill in the gaps.

In the past, grandparents, siblings, aunts, uncles, or cousins might have played this role. But most of us live and work too far away from our extended families for that to happen anymore. Friends must become family. When you're a working parent, especially one whose kids have outgrown simple day care or nanny situations but can't yet drive or take public transportation on their own, that network—your posse—is how you survive.

Here's how to build and use one effectively.

Engage

When you're managing a demanding job and busy kids, there's a tendency to be laser-focused on whatever task is at hand. At the office, you bang away at your projects, attend all your meetings, and eat at your desk; you don't have time for coffee room chitchat or lunch with colleagues. At school or activity drop-offs and pickups, you aim to be in and out; at classroom or birthday parties, you focus on your kids, not the other parents. While understandable, these strategies are misguided; they might save you some time in the short term, but they prevent you from building the relationships key to long-term success in your work-life juggle.

Most of my cubemates at HBR—and many of the colleagues with whom I work closely—are also working parents. We talk a great deal about our kids, not just their ages and grades but also their academic highs and lows, extracurriculars, personality quirks, likes and dislikes. We are closer colleagues because we share these stories—and more willing and able to help one another out. When I'm late for a podcast taping because I've had to deliver a forgotten backpack, I can text my co-host Dan, who has three kids, and our producer Curt, dad to a toddler, and they both understand. When I'm unexpectedly working from home because someone has come down with strep, my next-desk-over friend Amy, mom of two grown boys, emails me files with a sweet "I've been there" note.

In my personal life, I've learned to relish the moments I catch with other parents in the school lobby or on warm-weather evenings in the neighborhood playground. Even when I'm racing to the office or keen to get back to my laptop, I stop to check how people are doing, hear their news, and sometimes just hang out. I'll admit that when my kids were very little, I initially gravitated to other working mothers, thinking we'd have more in common. But I quickly learned that stay-at-home moms (and dads) could be close friends and amazing allies, too. When you engage with a broad swath of fellow parents, you widen everyone's circle of support.

Offer Your Help

This essay is about getting help, yes, but I recommend giving it first. As Wharton professor Adam Grant has documented, the people who are most successful at building networks and bolstering their careers as a result are those who offer their time, energy, and advice to others without expecting anything in return. Of course, this initial generosity starts a virtuous cycle of reciprocity. When we help people, they instinctively want to help us in return, and vice versa.

How does a busy working parent make time for that? When trying to connect with parents at your school or in your community, it can be as simple as offering to set up a post-practice carpool and handle the first run on an evening when you don't have to work late. Maybe you can't host an after-school playdate, but your sitter could, or you might volunteer to arrange one for the weekend. If your classroom parent is asking for people to contribute food and drinks for the next school get-together, sign up immediately for something easy like juice, napkins, or store-bought bagels.

On snow days in Boston, when schools are closed, my neighborhood friend Melanie, a realtor with three rowdy boys, employs this strategy: She immediately texts every boy mom within a half-mile radius (there are many scattered throughout our city streets) and offers to take their kids for the morning. If she's lucky, someone else—occasionally me—will volunteer for the afternoon. Sometimes, she keeps the crew for the whole day. But if she ever needs someone to babysit while she's showing a house or meeting a client, she has a dozen of us to call on.

At the office, simply treat your fellow working parents the way you would want to be treated. Encourage them to work from home when it makes their family lives easier. Cover for them when they need to leave early or come in late. Notice when they seem to be struggling and ask if there's anything you can do to help. Regularly offer words of encouragement and, when appropriate, advice.

Make the Ask

Many working parents, and particularly working moms, are keen to prove they can do it all. You don't want to seek out special treatment from your boss or colleagues or depend on other parents to take care of your kids. Abandon those notions. Get comfortable asking for help.

The first step is to understand that people like assisting others more than we realize, as psychologist Heidi Grant has noted. Often, they don't consider it a burden. In fact, it makes them feel good. Even if you haven't yet initiated the cycle of reciprocity I describe above, don't underestimate how willing most people (particularly fellow parents) are to lend you a hand.

My colleagues know that the best time to schedule meetings with me is during school hours because I've politely asked them to make that accommodation. It's not always possible, but they know I'd like them to try. On the home front, I used to feel guilty about help requests, especially at the last minute, but my posse responds so positively to every ask that I've stopped worrying about it. I send texts like these: "Just left the office so won't make pickup in time. Any chance you could grab E?" "Forgot the sitter is away today. Would you mind taking an extra kid after school?" "Anyone able to give J a ride?" And the answers are always: "Sure!" "No problem!" "I can!"

Learn from Others

My view is that there are no universal rules to follow because each kid, each parent, and each parent–child relationship is unique. But I do firmly believe that we become better working parents when we talk through our problems with others in the same position and listen to and learn from them.

The best piece of working-parent advice I think I've ever received came from my colleague and dear friend Scott, dad to two girls, five and eight years older than mine. I'd been worrying that, in what little time I had with my kids in the mornings and evenings, I was focused more on discipline than fun. I didn't want them to think of me as someone who was either absentee (when at the office) or a scold (when at home). Scott's response: "It's not your job to be their friend. Your job is to make them better people." I felt instantly reassured and have shared this wisdom with many others.

More recently, I was chatting with a dad whose son and daughter go to school with mine; he's also a pediatric cardiologist. We had a long conversation about middle schools, work, politics, climate change, and health care. He could tell I was stressed about many of these things and at the end of our conversation said something like: "You know, in my job and in the world, there are so many things I can't control. So I try to focus on those things I can."

None of us are dealing with exactly the same issues, but chances are your working-parent friends, in both your professional and personal worlds, have navigated similar ones or know other people who have. So observe them, talk to them, lean on them. These sessions can be impromptu, but consider also planning regular check-ins with the inner circle of your posse. Dan and I have had adjoining desks since we started at HBR 10 years ago, and any time we both have a free moment, we make sure to quickly catch up on work and family matters. Similarly, my friend of 20 years, Rebecca, a fellow writer-editor, *Financial Times* alum, and mom of two, and I aim for a weekly lunch, coffee, or walk to discuss what's going on in our lives.

Balancing a career and a family isn't something you must do alone or with only your partner. Create your own parenting posse. There's a reason it's a cliché; we do get by with a little help from our friends.

Adapted from content posted on hbr.org, March 4, 2020 (product #H05GEP).

17

Create Your Own Personal "Board of Directors"

by Priscilla Claman

Quick Takes

- Expand the team of people you turn to for professional advice and support

- Select representatives from all different aspects of your life

- Tap people you trust, who are interested in you and your family

- Identify folks with experience or perspectives to share

For most of us, the many roles we play in our lives do not fit into two neat compartments of work and home. Covid-19 brought this into high relief as our pets and families make mostly unintentional guest appearances during our workdays, from the cat that leaps onto your desk to inspect your laptop and join your video meeting to the squabble that erupts in the next room while you're on a conference call.

As the distinction between home and work evaporates, borrowing a classic concept from work—mentoring—can help you manage the large and small challenges you face in all aspects of your life. Our use of mentors at work has evolved over time from one senior-level mentor, giving advice and actively promoting the careers of their mentees, to a portfolio of mentors, a personal board of directors you consult with regularly to get advice and feedback to help you shape and direct your career.[1]

The mentor concept of a single source of information and support has no direct equivalent in modern family life. Gone are the days of leaning on Grandma for child-raising help and as an authority figure. Since families no longer tend to live in the same community and Grandma may still be working herself, developing a portfolio of mentors can help you at home as much as it does at work.

A board of directors, whether for corporate life, family life, or both, needn't be a complicated project. It doesn't need to meet (members don't even have to all live in your same time zone), and you don't need to officially invite your mentors to participate or even inform them about your board.

Consider expanding your professional board of directors to include resources that will help you tackle family issues. It should comprise people you trust, have an interest in you and your family, and have experience or perspective to share. You'll want to select a range of people from all different aspects of your life. Since each person has their own network of contacts, choosing folks whose networks don't overlap will make your interactions with them more beneficial.

Here are some suggestions of people to include and how they can help:

- **Someone who shares your family's goals.** This person will help you support your family ambitions. Committed teachers or coaches are possible resources. If you want your daughter to get a soccer scholarship to college, the right coach can cultivate your daughter's talent, recommend activities to help her improve her skills, help assemble a highlight reel, and ultimately write her a college recommendation. If your son is great at academics but lonely, his junior high drama teacher can help him develop confidence and friends as well as acting skills.

- **One or more work colleagues who have families.** These people can help with employer issues, such as how to ask for a raise, which departments are hiring, or which managers are sympathetic to working parents. You'll find these colleagues through casual conversation. Notice and comment on the family photos on a person's desk. Listen for folks who chat about their families at work in a way that you admire. Or, bring in pictures of your own to share at work.

- **Working parents of children the same age as yours.** You'll find lots of candidates organically through your children's schools or activities. These parents can help you through crises great and small, such as, "Should I allow my kid to get that app?" or "How do I help the kids accept our divorce?" These parents can help you find the up-to-date resources and referrals you need.

- **Working parents of children who are older than yours.** Connect with at least one mentor who has children who are a school farther along than yours. So if your kid is in elementary school, tap someone with a middle schooler. These mentors will give you a hint of what's coming as well as some optimism about the future. I asked my school-ahead mentor how she was managing as the empty nester I would become in a few years. "There are some compensations," she replied. "Like private time with my partner on Sunday afternoons."

- **Parents of younger children than yours.** These parents give you some perspective on what you and your family have already achieved as well as an opportunity to give back. Sharing the tactics that worked for getting your kid to do her homework may help the younger parent, too—whether it's the tactic or just the knowledge that your family has also struggled in this area. Helping a family with younger children is beneficial for you, too. It will remind you of the challenges you have faced and mastered. It's something to be proud of.

- **A parent you like and respect but who frequently disagrees with you.** There isn't a clear right way to handle most of what life hands working parents. When things are confusing and ambiguous, and you don't know how to act, a little disagreement from a source you respect can go a long way toward helping you understand what to do and why. I have a go-to relative for this kind of advice. Usually, 90% of the time I don't do what he suggests as the "only reasonable" thing to do. But the discussion always helps me think it through.

- **Someone who thinks you and your family are wonderful.** This person is a consistent cheerleader, maybe a grandparent or special aunt, someone your family is in regular contact with. These mentors see your potential and your future. They know you can get frustrated by the day-to-day, and they can remind you of the big picture. I remember when my husband and I were trying to assemble a simple swing set. My parents-in-law were kibitzing from lawn chairs. "These things are never easy to put together. But you're doing great! The kids are going to love it." They were right.

Once you've assembled your board of directors, stay in touch—and not just with holiday cards. Connecting on social media is the easiest and most fun to do. Pictures are wonderful ways to convey what you and your family are up to. But every so often, take an extra step to reach out to say thank you for their friendship and support. It's important. So is letting them know how their advice turned out. It doesn't have to be elaborate. Just an email saying, "I followed your advice and talked to her teacher. It really worked!"

But as all the writing on mentors will tell you, contributing your gifts in return is key to sustaining strong mentoring relationships. Pay it forward by contributing not just to your mentors but to their contacts and the professional or community organizations they support. Something as simple as donating to your mentor's charity walk or buying pecans to support their kid's school fundraiser. And if they help you with a reference to a great pediatrician, it's easy to pay them back with a tip about a job lead.

You probably already have friends or family whom you consult when you need to, so expanding them into a board of directors isn't difficult. It's only a matter of being intentional about it. With a little thought and effort, your board of directors will provide your working-family juggling act with resources, information, and emotional support, as well as a sense of perspective—the gift of a new way of thinking.

Adapted from "Working Parents, Your Family Needs a 'Board of Directors'," on hbr .org, July 8, 2020 (product #H0%Q4M).

18

Making Time for Networking as a Working Parent

by David Burkus

Quick Takes

- Reestablish old relationships
- Ask current contacts for introductions
- Connect over video calls
- Introduce existing contacts to one another

Networks matter for career success. They help you find people who can assist you with projects, refer you to new employers, and make connections to new and bigger opportunities. In a famous study by Ronald Burt, people who made efforts to improve their networks were 42–74% more likely to be promoted than those who didn't.[1]

Here's the challenge: Networks often seem to grow during after-hours activities, like happy hours, weekend off-sites, or faraway conferences. That poses a problem for most working parents. How do you meet new people if traveling to conferences is out of the question? How do you strengthen connections with colleagues after work if you need to hurry home for soccer practice? For many working parents, this problem doesn't get solved and their network growth ceases (and maybe even shrinks).

But being a working parent doesn't have to mean the end of a thriving network; it just means you have to get a bit more creative and deliberate. I should know. As the father of two preschool-aged children and the husband to an emergency room physician, relying on organic network growth from after-hours events just wasn't feasible. I had to get intentional. I examined a variety of methods based on network research in my book *Friend of a Friend.* Here are a few evidence-based techniques I've found that work for me, and that may help you.

Press pause on making new contacts

When your kids are small, finding time to make new contacts can be a challenge, but there's a wealth of opportunity and new information that can come from old friends and former colleagues—in social networking jargon, your "weak" or "dormant" ties. And because you're already connected, reestablishing the relationship and catching up should be faster than making new connections. Weak ties are often more valuable than new contacts anyway, the research suggests. Don't overdo it, but find one dormant tie per week to reach out to. Skim social media profiles for updates on their life you can use as a reason to connect or take 30 seconds to share a quick note when an article, video, or something else brings that person to mind.

Explore the fringes of your network

After you've reconnected with dormant ties, start exploring who's on the edges of your network by asking for introductions from those weak ties. Like old contacts, it's a more time-efficient way to connect, since there's an intermediary you both share. My favorite method was to ask multiple people, "Who do you know in ___?" with the blank being the industry, company, geography, or whatever I wanted to get connected to. When the same name kept appearing on different people's list, that was a strong signal it was time to connect.

Redefine face-to-face

When you want to get to know a person or reconnect with someone you know, think beyond the coffee or lunch date. Video technology means a high-fidelity face-to-face conversation can happen without either of you leaving the office or your home.

Practice introductions

One of the most powerful things you can do to strengthen your network involves not meeting new people at all, but instead connecting two contacts in your network to each other. You strengthen the network around you, provide value for both contacts, and become known as a generous person. And you can do it any time of day via email (but make sure both parties know your introduction is coming).

Use business travel wisely

There may be times when traveling for work is unavoidable, so make the most of your time away. If you're traveling to a conference, do some research ahead of time to find out who else is coming and schedule quick chats throughout the event—rather than hoping to meet some interesting people just milling around the coffee station. If you're traveling for a different reason, see if you can arrive a few hours early or stay a little longer and use that extra time to reconnect with other contacts. My personal rule is that the number of overnights matter, but the number of hours in the day do not, so I try to arrive the earliest I can and leave as late as possible to sneak in a few more meetings.

Talk to your parent friends about more than just kid stuff

Research on social networks suggests that your most valuable connections come from people with whom you share multiple contexts (called your multiplex ties). So examining non-kid interests, hobbies, and even work can lead to a stronger bond and more reasons to stay connected. Likewise, doing family events with your colleagues can be a valuable way to invest time in multiple areas of your life. One of my favorite moments from a recent family vacation in Washington, DC, was the time we spent walking through the national zoo with a work colleague and his family. We became closer friends and more valuable colleagues.

If these steps seem like a regular part of networking, that's because they are. We just don't always view them this way. There's far more to growing a thriving network than attending formal networking events, working the room, and hoping you meet new people. Much of the work of networking involves taking care of the network you already have and slowly expanding it through current contacts. It's tempting to think that can only happen at after-work events or at big gatherings, but the truth is much of it can be done from your office during work hours.

You don't have to find more time to do networking; you just have to fit networking into the time you have.

Adapted from content posted on hbr.org, May 23, 2018 (product #H04BMO).

Epilogue

To Infinity, and Beyond!

19

What I Learned About Working Parenthood After My Kids Grew Up

by Avivah Wittenberg-Cox

Quick Takes

- Refocus on professional priorities and dreams
- Enjoy your weekends and evenings
- Travel for work becomes an opportunity to explore

There are so many articles about the challenges and stresses of being a working parent. Let me, for a moment, shine a light on the pleasures that await you once your kids have grown up and left home— it comes faster than you think.

You've probably heard of the happiness U-curve of life.[1] All over the world, human happiness slumps between the ages of 30 and 50. Those marriage-parenting-eldercare-working years can be a tough slog, as many of us will admit to one another.

But what fewer parents will admit to is the thrill of being post-hands-on parenting. The delight of watching the kids you have adored, accompanied, and applauded for a couple of decades blossom into themselves—and leave you the freedom to do the same. The sudden, astonishing emptiness of time when all that's left to do is . . . work. The ability to refocus on professional priorities and dreams is an unexpected gift, and one we rarely plan for. In my 30s, I assumed I'd be retiring in my 60s. But today, at 56, I'm beginning to think I've only just begun.

For primary caregivers, this is a discovery and a liberation. It took me years to adjust to the fact that weekends and evenings were my own. I found myself checking my inbox, sure that I was forgetting I had to drive someone somewhere, proofread an essay, or learn some weird new teenage texting pattern. Instead, the white space freed in my brain unleashed a fount of creativity and opportunity. Now, I can glam up and go to a weekend matinee after a late Sunday brunch with my spouse. I feel so grown up! I can also travel the globe for work, guilt-free and nonstop. My semiretired husband occasionally joins me. Suddenly business travel becomes fun and exciting, rather than exhausting and aging.

Another surprising discovery: Your children often become very interesting—even inspiring—people. They do interesting work in interesting places, and you get to visit them. And the more professional they get, the more relevant they discover you become. Not only do your business networks come in handy, but so does just about everything you've ever learned about stuff—from accounting to leadership. There are few prizes greater than catching a glimmer of pride in your child's eyes. Nothing matches the way your kids look at you when they suddenly discover that you are actually, astonishingly . . . interesting. These are the moments that are worth every twinge of terrible-parent guilt you ever felt about missing that school play or skipping out on soccer practice.

All the million little doubts that small humans are expert at implanting in their parents' guilty hearts when they are young tend to evaporate into thin air when they are older and in need of knowledgeable advice, or a friend with a skill, or even better, a job offer. It's a very particular pleasure to remain relevant as your children age. To realize that they don't grow up and leave—they grow up and call. A lot.

This is, sadly, not always the case, of course. I know parents who stayed home, and parents who focused exclusively on work, and in my experience those relationships often seem more difficult. The parents want the kids to appreciate their sacrifices, but the kids didn't ask the parents to make them. Carl Jung saw it clearly: "Nothing has a stronger influence psychologically on children than the unlived life of the parent." There is a happy middle, and balance and moderation are never judged over a day or a year, but over the decades.

As lives lengthen, the post-kid decades are stretching out healthier and wealthier than ever before. Depending on the age of your parenting peak (I did the classic 30 to 50), the amount of time you have to contribute your talents is growing. People are "unretiring," returning to work after an attempt at conforming to old ideas of age.[2] They rediscover purpose and pleasure at work—when it isn't driven by the crushing pressure of full-time schedules or revenue maximization.

Looking back at my years of peak working parenthood, there are four things I wish it had been easier to remember when I was in the thick of things:

1. Don't sweat the small stuff. One bad week doesn't make you a bad parent. When they grow up, your kids probably won't even remember it.

2. Don't burn out being a perfectionist parent. Instead, invest sustainably and regularly in yourself and your kids.

3. Love them a lot, but keep your ambition focused on your own career, not theirs.

4. If you are married, love your spouse, and don't demote your relationship to the bottom of the priority pile. No one will thank you. Your kids are learning relationship skills from you. Inspire them.

We all want to be wise elders to our children. Who knew, though, that doing so could take dedication to something *other* than them? In the end, they are the ones who show us that they weren't enough.

Being a working parent can be hard. But as you get older, like many other things, it gets better and better.

Adapted from content posted on hbr.org, April 13, 2018 (product #H049TV).

NOTES

Chapter 5

1. Sulin Ba and Lei Wang, "Digital Health Communities: The Effect of Their Motivation Mechanisms," *Decision Support Systems* 55, no. 4 (2013): 941–947.

2. Emma E. A. Cohen et al., "Rowers' High: Behavioural Synchrony Is Correlated with Elevated Pain Thresholds," *Biology Letters* 6, no. 1 (2009).

3. Leo Babauta, "Review Your Goals Weekly," Zen Habits, n.d., https://zenhabits.net/review-your-goals-weekly/; Gina Trapani, "How to Write To-Do Lists That Work," *Harvard Business Review,* January 13, 2009.

4. Noah J. Goldstein, Steve J. Martin, and Robert B. Cialdini, *Yes! 50 Scientifically Proven Ways to Be Persuasive* (New York: Free Press, 2008).

Chapter 6

1. Bureau of Labor Statistics, "Employment Characteristics of Families Summary," April 21, 2020, https://www.bls.gov/news .release/famee.nr0.htm.

2. Joan C. Williams, Mary Blair-Loy, and Jennifer M. Berdahl, "Cultural Schemas, Social Class, and the Flexibility Stigma," *Journal of Social Issues* 69, no. 2 (2013): 209–234.

3. Heejung Chung and Tanja van der Lipee, "Flexible Working, Work-Life Balance, and Gender Equality: Introduction," *Social Indicators Research,* November 28, 2018, https://link.springer .com/article/10.1007/s11205-018-2025-x; Williams et al., "Cultural Schemas, Social Class, and the Flexibility Stigma," 210; Sylvia A. Hewlett and C. B. Luce, "Off-Ramps and On-Ramps: Keeping

Talented Women on the Road to Success," *Harvard Business Review*, March 2005.

4. P. Stone, "Opting Out: Challenging Stereotypes and Creating Real Options for Women in the Professions," Harvard Business School Research Symposium, 2013, http://www.hbs.edu/ faculty/conferences/ 2013-w50-research-symposium/ Documents/ stone.pdf.

5. Williams et al., "Cultural Schemas, Social Class, and the Flexibility Stigma," 210.

6. D. Burkus, "Everyone Likes Flex Time, but We Punish Women Who Use It," *Harvard Business Review*, February 20, 2017; Williams et al., "Cultural Schemas, Social Class, and the Flexibility Stigma," 224.

7. Chung and van der Lippe, "Flexible Working, Work-Life Balance, and Gender Equality."

8. M. Benton, "Executive Women: Creating a Good Life in a World of Social Saturation" (unpublished doctoral thesis, University of Twente, Enschede, The Netherlands, 2017), 33–34.

Chapter 9

1. Mojca Filipič Sterle et al., "Expatriate Family Adjustment: An Overview of Empirical Evidence on Challenges and Resources," *Frontiers in Psychology* 9 (2018): 1207.

Chapter 11

1. Susan Harkness, Magda Borkowska, and Alina Pelikh, "Employment Pathways and Occupational Change After Childbirth," Government Equalities Office, October 2019, https://assets .publishing.service.gov.uk/government/uploads/system/uploads/ attachment_data/file/840062/Bristol_Final_Report_1610.pdf.

2. Claudia Goldin, "A Grand Gender Convergence: Its Last Chapter," *American Economic Review* 104, no. 4 (2014): 1091–1119.

Chapter 12

1. "Uncovering Talent—A New Model of Inclusion," Deloitte, 2013, https://www2.deloitte.com/content/dam/Deloitte/us/Documents/about-deloitte/us-about-deloitte-uncovering-talent-a-new-model-of-inclusion.pdf.

2. Dan Aloi, "Mothers Face Disadvantages in Getting Hired, Cornell Study Says," *Cornell Chronicle*, August 4, 2005, https://news.cornell.edu/stories/2005/08/mothers-face-disadvantages-getting-hired-study-shows.

Chapter 13

1. "Raising Kids and Running a Household: How Working Parents Share the Load," Pew Research Center, November 4, 2015, https://www.pewsocialtrends.org/2015/11/04/raising-kids-and-running-a-household-how-working-parents-share-the-load/.

2. I studied 113 dual-career couples ranging in age from 26 to 63, with an even distribution among age groups. The majority of couples—76—were in their first significant partnership. Participants in the study came from 32 countries on four continents, and their ethnic and religious backgrounds reflected this diversity. At the time of the study, roughly 35% resided in North America, 40% in Europe, and 25% in the rest of the world. In 68 of the couples at least one partner had children. Eleven of the couples identified as gay, and the rest as straight. Just under 60% of the participants were pursuing careers in the corporate world. The others were spread roughly equally among the professions (such as medicine, law, and academia), entrepreneurship, government, and the non-profit sector.

Chapter 14

1. "The Rise of the Dual-Earner Family with Children," *Daily*, May 30, 2016, https://www150.statcan.gc.ca/n1/pub/11-630-x/11-630-x2016005-eng.htm.

Chapter 15

1. Family Caregiver Alliance and reviewed by Margaret Neal, PhD, "Work and Eldercare," October 2012, https://www.caregiver.org/work-and-eldercare.

Chapter 17

1. Priscilla Claman, "Forget Mentors: Employ a Personal Board of Directors," hbr.org, October 20, 2010, https://hbr.org/2010/10/forget-mentors-employ-a-person.

Chapter 18

1. Ronald S. Burt and Don Ronchi, "Teaching Executives to See Social Capital: Results from a Field Experiment," *Social Science Research* 36, no. 3 (September 2007): 1156–1183.

Chapter 19

1. Christopher Ingraham, "Under 50? You Still Haven't Hit Rock Bottom, Happiness-wise," *Washington Post*, August 24, 2017.

2. Paula Span, "Many Americans Try Retirement, Then Change Their Minds," *New York Times*, March 30, 2018.

ABOUT THE CONTRIBUTORS

DAISY DOWLING, Series Editor, is the founder and CEO of Workparent, the executive coaching and training firm, and the author of *Workparent: The Complete Guide to Succeeding on the Job, Staying True to Yourself, and Raising Happy Kids* (Harvard Business Review Press, 2021). She is a full-time working parent to two young children. She can be reached at www.workparent.com.

ALISON BEARD is a senior editor at *Harvard Business Review,* cohost of the *Dear HBR:* and *HBR IdeaCast* podcasts, and a grateful mom to two fabulous children, Jack and Ella, and a funny cat, Pickle, who are the lights of her life.

MICHELE BENTON, is a wife of 20+ years, mom to a teenage son and tween-age daughter, and president of lime LLC, a marketing strategy, capabilities, and performance consultancy. Fed up that society's message to working parents is "Embrace the Suck," she runs the blog and resource center BeSaturated.com to help contemporary professionals create a good life in today's global, social, and digital times. Follow her on Twitter @michelebphd.

DAVID BURKUS, according to his two boys, "makes books, gives talks, and takes care of us." He's the best-selling author of four books, including *Friend of a Friend: Understanding the Hidden Networks That Can Transform Your Life and Your Career* (Houghton Mifflin, 2018).

PRISCILLA CLAMAN is president of Career Strategies, Inc., a Boston-area firm offering career coaching to individuals and career management services to organizations. She is a contributor to the *HBR Guide to Getting the Right Job* (Harvard Business Review Press, 2012). She is also the mother of three, the grandmother of nine, and the supplemental parent to four dogs, two cats, a rabbit, a retired horse, and 11 baby chicks.

JACKIE COLEMAN is a former marriage counselor and has recently worked on education programs for the state of Georgia and as a classroom teacher for young children.

JOHN COLEMAN is a business executive and coauthor of *Passion and Purpose: Stories from the Best and Brightest Young Business Leaders* (Harvard Business Review Press, 2011). Jackie and John Coleman are married and have three young children.

SCOTT EDINGER, founder of Edinger Consulting, is a coauthor of the HBR article "Making Yourself Indispensable." He is the author of *The Hidden Leader: Discover and Develop Greatness Within Your Company* (AMACON, 2015) and the forthcoming *The Butterfly Effect: How Great Leaders Drive and Sustain Revenue Growth*. Follow him on Twitter @scottkedinger or on LinkedIn. As a dad of two daughters, he provides amateur-level support as a TikTok backup dancer, Instagram photographer, and drivers ed instructor.

STEWART D. FRIEDMAN, an organizational psychologist at the Wharton School, is the author of three Harvard Business Review Press books—*Parents Who Lead: The Leadership Approach You Need to Parent With Purpose, Find Your Career, and Create a Richer Life* (2020), *Leading the Life You Want: Skills for Integrating Work and Life* (2014), and *Total Leadership: Be a Better Leader, Have a Better Life* (2008). He founded the Wharton Leadership Program, the Wharton Work/Life Integration Project, and Total Leadership, a management consulting and training company. His three grown children work in education. He hopes his two grandchildren will help us heal our broken world.

AMY GALLO is a contributing editor at *Harvard Business Review* and the author of the *HBR Guide to Dealing with Conflict at Work* (Harvard Business Review Press, 2017). She writes and speaks about workplace dynamics. As the parent of a teenager, she spends a lot of time trying to figure out how to apply her own advice on difficult conversations at home. Follow her on Twitter @amyegallo.

CARRIE KERPEN is the cofounder and CEO of Likeable Media and the author of *Work It: Secrets for Success from the Boldest Women in Business* (TarcherPerigee, 2018). With three children ranging in age from high school to preschool, she spends her nonwork time alternating between college prep, TikTok dances, and episodes of *Sesame Street*.

REBECCA KNIGHT is a freelance journalist in Boston whose work has been published in the *New York Times*, *USA Today*, and the *Financial Times*. She is the mom of two tween-age daughters.

KRISTIN MCELDERRY is a management consulting executive who works with public sector and higher education clients to transform their business. Kristin is the proud mother of three children (ages 2, 4, and 6) and spends her nonwork time having spontaneous dance parties, gardening, and going on bike rides.

LIZ O'DONNELL is the founder of Working Daughter and author of *Working Daughter: A Guide to Caring for Your Aging Parents While Making a Living* (Rowman and Littlefield, 2019) and *Mogul, Mom, and Maid:*

The Balancing Act of the Modern Woman (Routledge, 2016). She is a working daughter-in-law, wannabe mogul, and mother and maid to two teens.

CAROLYN O'HARA is a writer and editor based in New York City. She's worked at *The Week*, *PBS NewsHour*, and *Foreign Policy*. Follow her on Twitter @carolynohara1.

JENNIFER PETRIGLIERI is an associate professor of organizational behavior at INSEAD and the author of *Couples That Work: How Dual-Career Couples Can Thrive in Love and Work* (Harvard Business Review Press, 2019). She is the mum of Pietro (11) and Arianna (10), and together they enjoy growing vegetables, jumping on their trampoline, and going for long bike rides.

LISA QUEST is a partner at Oliver Wyman, head of the public-sector practice for the U.K. and Ireland, and a visiting academic fellow at the London School of Economics. With two young boys, she divides her time between reading *Thomas the Tank Engine*, building forts, and drinking way too much coffee.

AVIVAH WITTENBERG-COX is CEO of 20-first, a global gender consulting firm, and the author of *Seven Steps to Leading a Gender-Balanced Business* (Harvard Business Review Press, 2014). She's also written a book on the implications of gender balance at home, *Late Love: Mating in Maturity* (Motivational Press, 2018). She lives in London with her sculptor husband and is occasionally visited by her two globe-trotting, gender-balanced children—a son and a daughter.

INDEX

accountability, 18, 50, 51–52

active commitment, 50. *See also* goals

advice

about job relocations, 85–86

from personal board of directors, 9, 173–179

aging parents, caring for, 151–159

alignment, 6–7, 17. *See also* building a meaningful career

alternating-career model, 146–147. *See also* dual-career couples

alternative work arrangements, 55–61, 63–68, 100–101, 105–106. *See also* flexible work

annual board meetings, for families, 49–50. *See also* goals

asymmetric support, 132–134. *See also* dual-career couples

AT&T, 87

authenticity, 17–20

balance. *See* work-life balance

Beard, Alison, 163–171

behavior patterns, 24–25. *See also* work-life balance

Benton, Michele, 55–61

board of directors, personal, 9, 173–179. *See also* support networks

boss

communicating with, 104

telling about departure, 91–97

boundaries, managing, 22–24, 76, 123–125

brainstorming, 24, 43, 145

Bridgespan Group, 25–26

budgets, 11, 13

building a meaningful career, 3–13

Burkus, David, 181–186

business travel, 184–185, 190

career goals. *See* goals

after parental leave, 99–106

reassessing, 104–105

setting clear, 101–102

career transitions

handling departures, 91–97

later-in-life, 134–136